AMBER BLACK

Redemptive Grace
Transparent reflections on God's goodness

CLAY BRIDGES
PRESS

Redemptive Grace
Transparent reflections on God's goodness

Copyright © 2021 by Amber Black

Published by Clay Bridges in Houston, TX
www.ClayBridgesPress.com

All rights reserved. No part of this publication may be reproduced, stored in a retrieval system, or transmitted in any form by any means, electronic, mechanical, photocopy, recording, or otherwise, without the prior permission of the publisher, except as provided for by USA copyright law.

Unless otherwise markered, Scripture quotations are taken from the Holy Bible, New International Version®, NIV®. Copyright © 1973, 1978, 1984, 2011 by Biblica, Inc.™ Used by permission of Zondervan. All rights reserved worldwide. www.zondervan.com The "NIV" and "New International Version" are trademarks registered in the United States Patent and Trademark Office by Biblica, Inc.™

Scripture quotations marked ESV are from The ESV® Bible (The Holy Bible, English Standard Version®), copyright © 2001 by Crossway, a publishing ministry of Good News Publishers. Used by permission. All rights reserved.

ISBN: 978-1-953300-79-9
eISBN: 978-1-953300-78-2

To my amazing husband, Brian, for being my partner in all things, for loving me and forever supporting me.

To Britney for being the biggest supporter of this project, and for being my personal cheerleader. This is in print because of you!

To my children, Cecely, Titus, Hannah, and Hannah Mae, for being all I ever wanted. You have given me the greatest gift of motherhood, and I am eternally grateful.

To my siblings, Andrea, Tyler, and Timothy, for being the ongoing source of entertainment, humor, and friendship.

To my parents, Mama and Dad, for showing unconditional love.

To my Daddy and Grandmama in heaven for laying a foundation for me. I hope I made you both proud.

Contents

Introduction	1
Mistakes	3
Music	17
Sickness	31
Mama Trauma	41
Daddy Issues	55
Details	67
Hard Work	77
Spiritual Discipline Work Plan	83
These Three Remain	87
Brotherly (and Sisterly) Love	99
Tainted Love	113
From Wife to Not	129
Redemptive Grace	145
References	155

Introduction

I have always loved to read and write. There isn't a book that I wouldn't peruse. I have tried my hand at poetry and fiction. I have found that my "happy place" is non-fiction rooted in transparency. There was a season in my life where I felt God called me to that—He called me to be open and honest. He has allowed me to have a life filled with experiences that have tried me, broken me, and built me. I believe we all have a story to share, and I have felt God ask me to share mine.

I view myself as an ambassador for Christ. The Lord has done so many amazing things in my world. He has walked with me through valleys and rejoiced with me on mountaintops. He has protected me from evil. He has allowed me to battle depression, grief, and anger. I believe He has done something in me that He longs to do for others. I believe He has prompted me to share my story to empower other people to share theirs.

The goal of this book (and of my life) is to encourage others and to point them to the loving, beautiful, awesome God I serve. He created each human for a purpose and with a purpose. He has glorious plans for our lives. He loves us deeply and truly. He is good. Sometimes, we just need a reminder. So, friend, this reminder is for you of His redemptive grace!

"My mouth will tell of your righteous deeds,
Of your saving acts all day long—
though I know not how to relate them all.
I will come and proclaim your mighty acts, Sovereign Lord;
I will proclaim your righteous deeds, yours alone.

Redemptive Grace

Since my youth, God, you have taught me,
and to this day, I declare your marvelous deeds."
—Psalm 71:15-17

"Let the redeemed of the LORD say so,
Whom He has redeemed from the hand of the enemy ..."
—Psalm 107:2

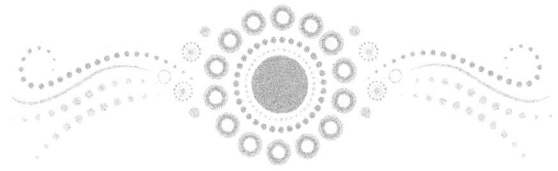

Mistakes

"[Lord] take away my desire to do evil or to join others in doing wrong…"
—Psalm 141:4a

I was a low-key little girl. I was theatrical and animated but never a discipline problem. I did not break the rules and rarely bent them. I wanted to please my parents and be a good role model to my three younger siblings. And, honestly, I was afraid of disappointing Jesus. When I was a child, I understood as a child. I did not understand the depth of my capacity for sin, nor did I grasp the unending, unconditional, gracious love of God.

I came to know Christ when I was six years old. I attended a small, Christian school during my elementary years. When I was in first grade, I remember deciding that I wanted to give my life to Christ. I was in Bible class listening to the teacher read about the brothers Cain and Abel (see Genesis 4). I recognized that I had sinned. I often thought mean things about my sister and brothers, and I sometimes acted on those thoughts. The issue of the sibling struggle between Cain and Abel struck a chord with me, and I was overwhelmed with the reality that I needed to be rescued from myself. I talked with my teacher, and she walked me through what God's Word said about sin and salvation. My parents had me follow-up with our pastor about my decision. I was baptized in October of 1987. I can vividly remember every step of the way from crying out in class, to the hugs and sweetness of my teacher, to the excitement of my parents, to the guidance of my pastor, to the thrill of baptism and to that feeling of joy that I did not fully understand. I have no doubt that I was saved when I was that little girl.

As I grew up, my family went through a series of exhausting events. There were strings of medical issues. There were constant financial burdens. There were the ups and downs of simply living life. My safe place was our church. We belonged to a sweet congregation of people who loved my family. We were always well ministered to during the trying times. We were included in fellowship. We were actively involved in almost every ministry of the church, and we were at the church all day every Sunday, each Wednesday night, and most Tuesday and Thursday afternoons. If we weren't physically at the church, our house was open to the people of the church, where my Mama often hosted meals and fun times! My first memories are of that church building. I can remember the white walls covered in construction paper crafts. I remember the musty smell of the small library that I visited every Wednesday. I remember the kind elderly ladies who insisted on giving my siblings and me candy. I remember the old men who wore flowers in their lapels on Sunday mornings. I still remember every Sunday School teacher and Children's Choir song. I loved my church.

When I was a teenager, I was the face of our youth group. I sang in the choir. I often had solos and made-up choreography for the music. I was on the youth council. I went out and witnessed with the bus ministry. I met my first love in the

Mistakes

youth group. During my younger years, I kept up my appearance of being the perfect person. My parents were proud. I had many friends. I like to think I was a cool big sister. People enjoyed being around me. My checklist to perfection was awesome. I was operating under a works-based salvation. Then, some changes started sneaking into our church. Conflict began. Gossip spread. Sides were formed. My church was no longer my safe place. As my parents took their stand, many of the people who had been so kind to our family no longer liked us. Many of my peers began to talk about my family. My Daddy would not leave the church, so we stayed for a while. I watched people be destroyed by other believers. I heard terrible exchanges where the only intent was to tear down others. I felt lost, confused, betrayed, and hurt. I clung to my boyfriend and blocked out everyone else.

I really did love my boyfriend. He was smart, funny, kind, and very romantic. My parents agreed to let me date at fifteen because of my record of stellar behavior … they trusted me. Over and over, I had proven myself responsible. They also had a very good relationship with my boyfriend's family, and his record of awesomeness rivaled mine. I completely believed this was the man I was going to grow up to marry. He and I would sing together at church. We would watch movies. He introduced me to the wonderful world of parody and satire as well as Broadway. He was a major contributor in teaching me to drive. He was a little older than I was. When he graduated high school and I still had two years left, he chose to give up going to a college out of town, and he stayed locally for me. He helped care for me when I was sick. He showered me with thoughtful gifts. He protected me. He wrote me love notes. He wasn't perfect, but he was pretty amazing.

While I was dating this young man, I finally learned how messed up I was. I got a huge dose of reality as to how deep I could sin, how far I could fall. I want to be very clear and transparent that my boyfriend never asked me or made me do anything I didn't want to. I physically craved his attention and touch. I began to lie. At first, I would get sick to my stomach with each falsehood. As time passed, lying to my family and friends became so easy. It started by lying about where I was, and who I was with. This was long before the time of cell phones. Like I said, my parents trusted me. Why wouldn't I be where I said I was? All my lies circled around my desire for sexual intimacy. I willingly became sexually active when I was fifteen years old. I only committed this act with my boyfriend, which helped me justify my behavior. After all, I loved him, and we had plans for a future together. I lied to my Mama so she would take me to the doctor. I lied to the doctor so she would give me birth control pills. I lied to my friends. Only a few knew the truth. When I trusted the wrong people, I became a topic of gossip for church teens. Oh, how I had fallen. No, how I had jumped! While I did not fully understand the long-term ramifications of giving up my purity, I did understand that I was doing wrong.

While the church I loved was separating, while my parents were fighting hard battles, while I was consistently seeking physical attention, I was slinking farther and farther away from God. I had stopped praying. I had stopped reading my Bible. I began to perform. For the sake of my parents and

Mistakes

siblings, I kept up the act of perfection. I felt the only person who truly knew me and understood me was my boyfriend. He and I made up our own reality and avoided the truth. My heart was so heavy with my sin. I began to develop a selfish streak. Now, my boyfriend wasn't enough. He wasn't perfect, but he was very good to me. In my selfishness and dominating desire to be valued for my body, I decided to break up with him. I immediately began dating another young man at the church my family had begun visiting. At this point, I had the lowest opinion of myself. I confided in the new boyfriend about my past struggles. I was battling wanting to be restored. Under the guise of care, my new boyfriend reminded me I was fortunate that he wanted me given that I had already given away my virginity. That relationship was the shortest yet most destructive relationship of my life. I broke up with the new guy. I wanted something better. I wanted to be better.

I had made friends with a brother and sister at school who had started attending the church my family had moved to. We spent a lot of time together. I was not dating anyone, and I knew the brother was interested in me. In their eyes, I was this pristine girl who sang in concerts and was on homecoming court. In my search for finding peace and redemption, I told them about my past. What happened next was one of the most trying times of my teen years. My friends told their parents what I had told them. Their father began calling and leaving messages on my family's answering machine. Terms like "slut" and "whore" were left for my unsuspecting parents and my innocent siblings to hear. My parents were infuriated. I remember one Sunday when my Daddy verbally attacked their father calling him a liar after he told my parents they had raised a

Redemptive Grace

"tramp" who was not welcome near his children. The pressure of my pain was intense. I felt isolated. I had removed myself from fellowship with the God who had saved me when I was a little girl. I had distanced myself from my parents, brothers, and sister. I had very few peers left who truly knew me. The weight of my choices was breaking my spirit.

Thankfully, this new church had an excellent youth pastor. He and his wife were friendly, honest, and wonderful people. Their home was always open to teenagers. I attended church because I had to … I needed to keep up appearances. They were abundantly kind to m)e. I called them up and asked if I could come talk with them. When I arrived at their home, they were both standing at the door. We came into the house with the Weather Channel playing in the background and bread baking in the oven. They sat on the sofa, and I sat cross-legged on the floor in front of them. I told them everything. I was afraid they wouldn't want me in their home or near their daughter anymore. The opposite was true. The wife wept with me and held my hands. The youth pastor put his hands on my shoulders and prayed out loud for me. They both held me tight. They opened up the Bible and read to me the truth! I had given into lies and given up so much. I wasn't sure what the truth was anymore. In their kindness, they also offered to mediate a meeting between my parents, siblings, and me.

I will always remember the day I confessed my sins to my parents. My Daddy was furious. His face turned bright red. He yelled and screamed at me. I had hurt him deeply. His perfect little girl no longer existed. My Mama never raised her voice. She just lowered her eyes. She cried in the

Mistakes

heartbreak of knowing my purity had vanished. She told me I had broken her trust. My sister and brothers were saddened but they did not fully understand (at that time) the gravity of what I had told them. I knew there would be consequences for my actions. I knew I would be punished for my wrongdoing. I will say this—even with the depth of my sin, my parents were very gracious and loving in their discipline.

I share this time in my life for several reasons. First, God is so good. His presentation of love is so deep while being so simple. Even as a six-year-old child, I understood that I had done wrong, I needed a savior, and that God had given Jesus to save me. I did not understand that the weight of my sin would grow to be more than I could imagine. I did not believe that God's goodness and love was greater than my sin. I want you to know that He loves you, too! No matter what you've done or will do!

Secondly, I want to remind you that we are all messed up. I'm a disaster. You're a mess. Confession is good for the soul; actually, confession with discretion is good for the soul. If you are holding onto a secret sin, if you are facing a battle, if you are weighed down by your choices, please find a safe, trustworthy person who can walk with you and point you towards the truth found in God's Word and through His Son. This is an appropriate place to remind you that confession is not meant to be shared to the world—so, avoid social media! Protect yourself and be wise.

Finally, I want to remind you of the reality of the enemy. Satan's goal is to destroy lives and claim them as his own. He wants you to feel alone. He wants you to pull away from God,

Redemptive Grace

the Truth, and those who love you. He wants the burden of your sin to crush you. There is no one without sin. The only human to have lived a sinless, blameless, perfect life was Jesus Christ. Each one of us will daily have to fight the battle against ourselves and the sin within. So, ready yourself to fight! Set aside frequent time to have conversations with the One who created you. Make time to be in His Word, which is the TRUTH!

Your sinful nature is a part of you, but it is not all of you. Let it go. Confess it to God. Confide in a trusted, Christ-centered friend. Pray … all day, every day! Clear your heart and mind of the wrongdoing and allow God to fill those spaces with His grace, goodness, and limitless love.

Now it's your turn. Let's get to work!

When I taught with the Good News Club, the curriculum stated that sin is "anything we think, say or do that is against God's Word" (Child Evangelism Fellowship, 2019). Write out what the word "sin" means to you.

_____

_____

Romans 3:10 says, "none is righteous, no, not one … ." In verse 23 we read, "for all have sinned and fall short of the glory of God." Further on in Romans, the Bible says "for the wages (payment) of sin is death …" in chapter 6, verse 23. In your own words, explain what these passages say about sin.

Mistakes

_____

_____

_____

What is your sin struggle? We all deal with something. I sin everyday whether it is in gossip, losing my temper, thinking unkind thoughts, reacting to a situation inappropriately. The sin I have struggled with, have fought with since my teen years is defining my worth by physical intimacy. With God's guidance and the accountability of my husband and a close friend, I have placed parameters in my life to help me fight my sin nature and to protect myself, my marriage, and my testimony. Think about your life. What has been your "thing?" What is the issue that requires your attention? If you are not sure, ask God to reveal it to you. Write it down. Confess it to your Maker.

_____

_____

_____

_____

What are some guardrails you can put in place in your life to help you fight this battle?

_____

_____

_____

Redemptive Grace

_____

_____

_____

In our culture, it is very easy to justify our sins. We can always find a person or situation to blame. While our circumstances can influence our decisions, the decision to sin still rests in the power of the individual. Think about your life. Is there a situation where you failed but that you have not owned? Is there someone or something that you are blaming rather than taking on your own indiscretion? Confess it! Ask God to reveal areas in your life where you have (or may still be) justifying your failure. "In you Lord, I take refuge; let me never be put to shame. In your righteousness, rescue me and deliver me; turn your ear to me and save me" Psalm 71:1-2. There is freedom in the truth! There is power in releasing blame and letting go of shame!

_____

_____

_____

_____

_____

"Let not sin therefore reign in your mortal body, to make you obey its passions. Do not present your members to sin as instruments for unrighteousness but present yourselves to

Mistakes

God as those who have been brought from death to life, and your members to God as instruments for righteousness. For sin will have no dominion over you, since you are not under law but under grace" (Romans 6:12-14, ESV). How can you apply this passage in your life?

_____

_____

_____

_____

_____

_____

_____

_____

When you decide to follow Jesus, you will still have to fight your sinful-self daily, but you will be fighting with Jesus on your side! You will be able to fight with the confidence of one who has been brought from the death of sin to life with Christ! Have you made that decision? If you have, I am so happy and look forward to meeting you one day in Heaven. If you haven't, please consider Jesus. To choose to follow Him is simple. Admit to God that you recognize yourself as someone who sins. Believe that God sent His Son, Jesus to pay the price for every sin you have ever committed and every sin you have yet to commit. Confess your sins to Him. Connect with

Redemptive Grace

a Bible-believing, Gospel-centered church that can help you start this new journey to TRUTH!!! Need some help getting started? Read Psalm 141 and be inspired by David's words.

"I call upon you, O Lord; come quickly to me. Hear my voice when I call to You. May my prayer be set before You like incense, my uplifted hands like the evening offering. Set a guard, O Lord, over my mouth; keep watch at the door of my lips. Do not let my heart be drawn to any evil thing or take part in works of wickedness with men who do iniquity; let me not feast on their delicacies. ... But my eyes are fixed on You, O God the Lord. In You I seek refuge; do not leave my soul defenseless..."

—Psalm 141

Use the following space to write a prayer to God. This can be a prayer of confession, thanksgiving, questions ... whatever, just get your words on paper!

_____

_____

_____

_____

_____

_____

_____

_____

Mistakes

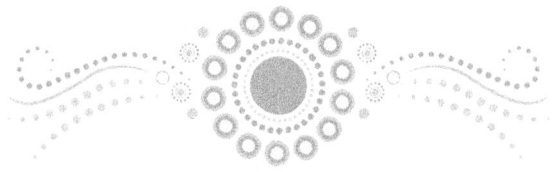

Music

"Let the word of Christ dwell in you richly, teaching and admonishing one another in all wisdom, singing psalms and hymns and spiritual songs, with thankfulness in your hearts."
—Colossians 3:16

Do you remember your senior year of high school? Did you love it? Did you hate it? Maybe you haven't gotten to that milestone yet. If that's the case, take some advice from me and enjoy that last year of high school! While I began my educational journey in a small, Christian school, I transitioned to public school in sixth grade and continued through my twelfth-grade year. I really loved school. I was a complete nerd in that my grades were the most important thing to me. I took the most challenging English and history classes. I hated math, so I took what I had to, then kept it easy with SAT Prep my senior year. I wanted that perfect GPA and those winning SAT scores. The goal was to go to college and to hopefully have it paid for.

I also allowed time for fun by taking a theater class, where I was thrilled to play Addaperle in The Wiz. I had been in school chorus since sixth grade. I sang at church in the youth choir. I was also fortunate enough to travel with my Daddy to sing at churches for homecomings, weddings, and funerals. I loved music. My parents had forced my siblings and me to take piano lessons while we were in elementary school. We did not like those lessons, BUT I am so thankful for what I learned by taking piano that helped shape me as a vocalist. I have always loved music.

When I was young, the only music in our home was Christian. My Daddy loved Southern Gospel; so, the Gaithers, the Goodmans, the Kingsmen, Jake Hess, and Dottie Rambo were celebrities in our home. My Mama enjoyed what was then called "contemporary" Christian music including Michael W. Smith, Steven Curtis Chapman, Sandi Patti, and the rebel of them all, Carman. As I entered middle school, I was allowed to listen to bands like Point of Grace, Four Him, and the ever-edgy D.C. Talk. At school, I was singing Latin, French, and German arias. Occasionally, I would hear secular music in a store or a friend's car, but since these songs weren't familiar to me, they didn't stick in my head. As I grew older, I was exposed to more music genres. I spent several weekends at my friend's home where their cousins would come over and play the latest country tunes or big hair bands from the 1980s. I had another friend who had a big brother who was all about the grunge scene (thank you 1990s). One friend was into alternative rock. Another friend was all about female hip-hop artists. My Daddy had a secret stash of classic rock vinyls that I discovered and fell in love with. The more styles of music I heard, the more I realized the love of music that was embedded in me, and the more grateful I was to have been gifted with musical ability.

I absolutely loved singing. I was sharing my expanding musical knowledge with my siblings. My sister latched on to the R&B melodies and boy band hype. My brothers were

Music

drawn to classic rock, country and even some showtunes. In my world, music brought fun and a little bit of rebellion. (Side note-my Mama was not a fan of my growing musical information. I would hide cassette tapes from her that my friends made for me. If she found one, she made me listen to it with her then tell her what the song meant line by line. That happened with Boyz 2 Men and Salt-N-Pepa. I became more discreet in my listening habits!)

During the first semester of my senior year, I started having problems with my voice. When I was growing up, I would always lose my voice in the fall and spring for a few days, and my doctor related it to allergies. The first few times this happened to me as a senior, I didn't panic; I assumed it was an allergy thing. My voice loss became more persistent. I could be reading out loud in English class at full volume, then my voice would just disappear—not fade, just stop. Singing became a game of chance. Maybe I would be able to hit those first soprano notes or maybe I wouldn't be able to even hit the tenor line. I didn't have any pain, just frustration. I went to my regular doctor who sent me to an ear, nose, and throat doctor. After a series of disgusting tests where tubes were stuck up my nose and down my throat, acid reflux was ruled out along with any bronchial or allergy issue. He determined I had polyps or nodules. I was referred to a specialist in a city a few hours away from my home. My initial visit was to establish my routines and to see if any patterns could be detected with my symptoms.

Over the next few months, I underwent a variety of tests. My Mama always went with me to these appointments, and my Daddy would come when he could. The first test was again having a tube placed up my nose, down my throat and hooked to a monitor. This had to be left on for twenty-four hours and required me to take on normal activities while it was in place. I had to talk, sing, eat, etc. all the while feeling this tube that felt as thick as a garden hose in my throat. I would sing and gag, eat and choke. My Mama would encourage me a lot and cry a little. We found out that I had developed cysts up and down my vocal cords. The next test was gruesome. I was taken into an examination room and laid out flat. I could not have any anesthesia on my neck because the test was to watch how my vocal cords would react. Nine needles were placed into my throat, one at a time. With each needle, I could feel the metal move around inside my throat, cold and foreign. As each needle was added, I was asked to read a passage out loud or sing a few lines from a song. These needles were about ten inches long because they had to be able to go through the layers of the throat to reach the vocal cords while being manipulated by the nurse or doctor externally. The process of this test was brutal. The pain is one I still am not sure how to properly describe. After this, my neck was bruised and swollen, but the next day, I was back at school.

After several less-exciting procedures and countless more days of having no voice, it was decided that I would have a bilateral medialization—translation: my throat would be cut open for the doctor to see my vocal cords with his own eyes. Fun fact, I would be awake for this and would be without any anesthesia again, just a topical cream for my neck where the incision would be made. When I arrived for this appointment, I was very scared. However, God has blessed me with

Music

a weird sense of humor, so I had jokes at the ready for my doctor. As we entered the operating room, he allowed me to choose what music we would listen to during the procedure; this was also to encourage me to sing during the procedure. I chose Broadway hits and off we went! My doctor had an enormous ego, but he was very kind and funny. During the procedure, he kept me giggling. I can remember the feel of the chilly knife that cut the incision in my throat. I can remember the weight of the tools used to move the parts of my throat out of the way. I remember seeing and feeling the clips that would hold my throat open. I remember the constant feeling of choking throughout the surgery. I remember singing "All I Ask of You" from Phantom of the Opera while the doctor poked, pulled, and searched for an answer.

It felt like hours, but I know it wasn't, until I felt my throat being stitched up by the nurse. A huge layer of gauze was wrapped around my neck and another layer of material added to keep my neck stable. I was given strict instructions on the limitations of neck movement for the next few weeks along with the command of complete vocal rest for six weeks. In the recovery room, my parents and I were told that my doctor had figured it all out. During the procedure, he had discovered that my left vocal cord was completely paralyzed. I kept having nodules, polyps and cysts reappear because my right vocal cord was doing the work of both. With my constant singing, I was putting that one cord on a constant Marine-worthy workout! The resolution was to place a silicone implant in the left vocal cord to fatten it up and give the right vocal cord less ground to cover. I immediately wrote the comment to the doctor that I finally had implants … well, just the one. My Mama hated when I told that joke later … sorry, Mama!

After the vocal rest, I would be allowed to talk an allotted amount of time a day, but I would not be allowed to sing for the remainder of the semester. My chorus teacher was kind enough to let me stay in the chorus, and I became the page-turner for him as he played the piano. He was also extremely gracious along with my drama teacher, to allow me a small part in the spring musical. I had committed to singing at high school graduation with a friend, and I was self-conscious through the entire ceremony. It would be several years before I would sing again outside of my home. My first soprano voice had changed to a second alto. I was extremely self-conscious of my ability. I felt I had lost my gift. I did not sing in public again for at least five years when I joined the choir and worship team for the church I attended. My voice wasn't the same, but the love I had for song never diminished.

When I was younger, I struggled with why God would let this happen to me. I didn't understand why He would take away a gift He had given me that I often used to give Him glory. I didn't understand why He had me go through the painful tests and surgery. None of it made sense. I was still struggling with understanding God's grace and was living in a works-based mindset. I thought maybe my voice was taken from me because of my sin. As I grew older and a little bit wiser, I realized that the real issue was my pride. I liked the way I sounded. I enjoyed the compliments from others. I didn't really want to be on the stage unless I was singing. My confidence had crossed over to arrogance. I often had the focus on me—the glory was not being given to God. I was

Music

keeping it for myself to fuel my ego and to make myself feel better about the hidden sins in my life. I was a performer. Inside, I was cut off from God, per my decision; outside, I was an actor playing a role. My heart was corrupt. My need to find approval in my talent was not fulfilling me, it was making the lies deeper, and I was drowning in my false persona. I don't have the answer, but I wonder if God allowed this part of my story to help me take the focus off of me. I think it was a steppingstone of breaking my façade and revealing my need for a renewed relationship with my Savior.

One of my favorite songs is Keith and Kristyn Getty's version of "In Christ Alone" (Getty & Townsend, 2002). There is so much truth in this song concerning who God is, the price Jesus paid, and who we are in Christ. (You can find this song online and often hear it on Christian radio stations.) The last verse resonates in my heart, and when I sing it, I almost forget my Southern Baptist upbringing and want to dance! Please look it up and give it a listen. The lyrics speak to the fact that there is nothing that can happen to you that Jesus does not know about. Nothing that can happen that will surprise Him. Nothing where He will let you out of His hand. Nothing. You are His. Say that out loud, "I am His!" If you don't have a song that speaks to you the way this one does to me, I'll let you share this one with me. I would encourage you to search out the lyrics of a song that is rooted in Biblical truth and points you to Jesus. Let it be a song that helps lift you up when you are down. Write the lyrics to your song of choice below.

_____

_____

Redemptive Grace

_____
_____
_____
_____
_____
_____
_____
_____
_____
_____
_____
_____
_____
_____
_____
_____
_____

Still need help finding a go-to song? Check out the book of Psalms. This beautiful book in the center of the Bible was written "to provide poetry for the expression of praise, worship, and confession to God" (Zondervan, 2011). There are

Music

many authors in this book with David being the primary writer. I love Psalms. When I am out of words to pray or my heart is so heavy, I can't form my own sentences, I go to the Psalms and use David's words.

Now it's your turn. Let's get to work!

Is there a time in your life where you faced a trial you did not understand? What happened?

_____

_____

How did you feel?

_____

_____

_____

What was your relationship with God like during this time?

_____

_____

_____

Being a follower of Christ does not mean that we will not have trials. It means that when we inevitably face problems, we have amazing resources on our side. We have an

Redemptive Grace

all-knowing, all-seeing, Father God who is holding our world in His capable, strong hands. We have a savior in Jesus who faced trials and who is praying on our behalf. We have the Holy Spirit residing in us connecting us to Jesus and speaking to our innermost being. We have God's Word that is full of wisdom. We have the power of prayer—having communication with God. We have a community of believers to support us if we ask them. We are not alone!!! YOU ARE NOT ALONE!!!

Psalm 103 is a beautiful song jam-packed with truth about the God we love and serve. This is one of my favorite psalms. Read it section by section. After each block of verses, write what these words mean to you.

Verses 1-5
"Bless the Lord, O my soul; all that is within me, bless His holy name. Bless the Lord, O my soul, and do not forget all His kind deeds—He who forgives all your iniquities and heals all your diseases, who redeems your life from the Pit and crowns you with loving devotion and compassion, who satisfies you with good things, so that your youth is renewed like the eagle's."

_____

_____

_____

_____

_____

Music

Verses 6-10
"The Lord executes righteousness and justice for all the oppressed. He made known His ways to Moses, His deeds to the people of Israel. The Lord is compassionate and gracious, slow to anger, abounding in loving devotion. He will not always accuse us, nor harbor His anger forever. He has not dealt with us according to our sins or repaid us according to our iniquities."

_____

_____

_____

_____

Verses 11-14 (my favorite chunk)
"For as high as the heavens are above the earth, so great is His loving devotion for those who fear Him. As far as the east is from the west, so far has He removed our transgressions from us. As a father has compassion on his children, so the Lord has compassion on those who fear Him. For He knows our frame; He is mindful that we are dust."

_____

_____

_____

_____

_____

Redemptive Grace

Verses 15-19

"As for man, his days are like grass—he blooms like a flower of the field; when the wind passes over, it vanishes, and its place remembers it no more. But from everlasting to everlasting the loving devotion of the Lord extends to those who fear Him, and His righteousness to their children's children—to those who keep His covenant and remember to obey His precepts. The Lord has established His throne in heaven, and His kingdom rules over all."

_____

_____

_____

_____

Verses 20-22

"Bless the Lord, all His angels mighty in strength who carry out His word, who hearken to the voice of His command. Bless the Lord, all His hosts, you servants who do His will. Bless the Lord, all His works in all places of His dominion. Bless the Lord, O my soul!"

_____

_____

_____

_____

How can you apply this passage to your life?

_____

_____

Music

_____

_____

As you look ahead, knowing troubles will come, what are some action steps you can put in place to remind you of who God is and who He can be in your life?

1. _____

_____

2. _____

_____

3. _____

_____

_____

_____

_____

_____

_____

_____

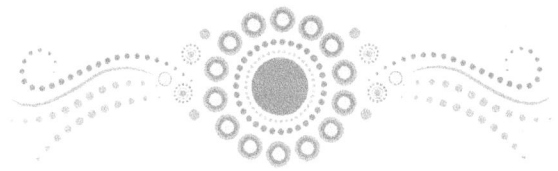

Sickness

"When you pass through the waters, I will be with you; and when you pass through the rivers, they will now sweep over you. When you walk through the fire, you will not be burned..."
—Isaiah 43:2

When I was going with my Daddy to sing at homecomings at local churches, one of my favorite songs to sing was "When You Walk Through the Water" (originally performed by Allison Durham Speer. Look it up and take a listen!). This song is based on the above Scripture, and it became a prophetic tune in my life. As I began to grow up and mature in my faith, I truly believed that God was always with me. He had protected me from myself in my youth. He had granted me peace and humor during my vocal cord ordeal. I had several opportunities to be burned or drowned, but He had always delivered me.

As my senior year of high school began to wind down, a new season of medical misfortune started up. I was never an athletic person. I ran one season on indoor track just so I could earn the letter and have it on my resume for college applications (ever-battling a performance-based existence). While I wasn't sporty, I did take care of myself and was a healthy teenager. I was average height and weight. I didn't eat crazy portions. My exercising was dancing or running around with my siblings. I started to notice my abdomen swelling from time to time. My belly would stick out, and I couldn't button my pants. I began to have intermittent episodes of intense pain. I would feel my stomach burning. It literally felt as if there was a fire blazing. Eventually, I started losing blood. I would have no energy or strength. I remember going to my doctor and him saying to me as he listened to my belly with his stethoscope, "it sounds like a herd of elephants running through your gut."

At this point, I had begun my college journey. I was attending school a whopping nineteen miles away from my parents' home. I came home every weekend. I came to town during the week to doctor appointments as another round of testing, ultrasounds, and scans began. I had also become engaged to my boyfriend of two years. My Grandmama, Mama, sister and myself were planning my simple wedding. Then, the weight started falling off. My Grandmama was making my wedding dress, and at every fitting, she would have to take it in. I had started to have frequent emergency room visits that turned into overnight observations. It was finally determined that I had Crohn's Disease. I will spare you the super-glamorous details because I don't want to promote a spirit of jealousy (wink-wink).

Crohn's Disease is an auto-immune disease that can take up residence anywhere in the digestive tract. It can stay in one place, or it can move around. Crohn's Disease can look very different in each case. It can also change a lot in a single patient. For me, it materialized in constant pain, losing several cups of blood a day, unhealthy weight loss, extreme lethargy, abdominal swelling, and fiery pain. I will say a "bonus"

Sickness

to this condition was it scored me a private room my second and third semesters of college! As I was planning a wedding, taking a full course load at school, and preparing to make a big move away from my small-town home to the big city of Chicago, it was safe to say I was overwhelmed. In the nights when I would pass out in the bathroom and wake up to my parents or siblings dragging me to my bedroom, I would battle fear. When I would have to miss a class and tell the professor why I was out, I would struggle with humiliation. Who wants to talk to their teacher about digestive tract issues? When I would think ahead to moving and dealing with these issues without my family, I would entertain worry. When I realized the financial costs of hospital visits and medication, I would welcome anxiety.

During this time of transition and joy and stress, I would be tempted to forget God's steadfast love. Again, I would ask why me? Why now? For what purpose? On my wedding day, the ceremony started late because I was stuck in the bathroom waiting for an episode of sickness to pass. For two weeks before the wedding, all I could consume was Gatorade. My body simply would not digest food. I was passing out every other day. The morning of the ceremony, my family and I arrived to decorate the chapel and reception hall. When it was time to get ready, I was ushered to the bathroom, and I just sat there. I don't remember much. I am thankful pictures were made so that I could look back, but I don't like the pictures because I don't look like a blushing bride; I look like a shell of a girl. My family and friends dolled me up. They helped me get dressed. Someone stayed in the bathroom stall with me, holding my dress for I don't know how long as I dealt with a flare-up. My Mama and Daddy walked me down the aisle and lovingly handed me over to my soon-to-be husband. My memories of the ceremony are fuzzy. I don't remember the reception at all.

Following the reception, my new husband had to take me directly to the hospital where I was instantly admitted. The first nurse came into my room to get the IVs started. She looked at me with my makeup and fancy hair and began to cry. I looked her straight in the eye and told her she was not coming near me with a needle. It did not make sense to me that I was the calm one in the room! Another nurse came in to get me plugged up to fluids. Then, a steady stream of visitors came into the room. To say the honeymoon was intimate or magical would be a lie; to say it was vastly expensive would be correct. However, I distinctly remember hearing the Lord speak to me as I laid in the hospital bed on my wedding day. He told me to "shine." Guests from the wedding and hospital staff would be coming in and out of my room for the next two days. This was a chance for me to share God's goodness.

Yes, I was physically miserable. I was sick and puny. I was tired and distraught. I was scared and worried. BUT I was still holding on to my Savior. Jesus was my lifeline. As people would come to check on me, I would make them smile with a crazy comment or silly joke. If they asked me how I could be laughing in this circumstance, I would say, "it's not me. It's Jesus in me." My joy was real and not my own. While I was not at all perfect or handling things with confidence, I was still clinging to Jesus. I was able to share some of His light in

Sickness

one of my most uncomfortable times. The nurses joined in my humor, and on my day of discharge, they lined up outside the hospital and tossed Cheerios (they didn't have rice) for my husband and me as we left. I do think that is a precious memory.

Over the next few years, my Crohn's Disease symptoms would go up and down. I would have seasons of remission where I finally felt like my energetic self. I would take medications that cost thousands of dollars a month only to develop painful side effects. I would take the affordable option of steroids that would slow inflammation but cause my face and extremities to swell up beyond recognition. I would get to spend time in hospitals all over while moving wherever the Navy sent my husband. Throughout the medical hardships, God was faithful. I was often alone while my husband was in training or on deployment. I was far from home. I had to handle things independently. I actually wasn't independent at all; I was completely dependent on God. In all the quiet time I had, I would read His Word. I would listen to songs that reminded me of His faithfulness, goodness, and control. I would talk to Him.

A passage that I read over and over during these times is the one I mentioned at the beginning of this section. "But now, this is what the LORD says—He who created you, O Jacob, he formed you, O Israel: "Fear not, for I have redeemed you; I have summoned you by name; you are mine. When you pass through the waters, I will be with you; and when you pass through the rivers, they will not sweep over you. When you walk through the fire, you will not be burned; the flames will not set you ablaze" Isaiah 43:1-2. In these verses, the Lord is talking to His chosen people, the Israelites. He was reminding them that He made them. He was offering them comfort. He was not telling them He was going to keep them from the surging waters or raging fires. Instead, He is commanding them to not fear because He will be with them in the water and the fire! He is telling them no matter the battle ahead, He will be with them.

When is a time when you have been worried? Afraid? Anxious?

_____

_____

_____

_____

_____

How did you cope?

_____

_____

Just like the children of Israel, we need to be reminded of God's faithfulness, and the command we have as His children to fear not! God does not say, "come to me, and I will make your path easy." He does say "fear not" because He will walk with you! Read the following verses and rewrite each one in your own words.

Sickness

"Be strong and courageous. Do not be afraid or terrified because of them, for the LORD your God goes with you; He will never leave you nor forsake you."
—Deuteronomy 31:6

_____

_____

_____

_____

"Have I not commanded you? Be strong and courageous. Do not be afraid; do not be discouraged, for the LORD your God will be with you wherever you go."
—Joshua 1:9

_____

_____

_____

_____

"When I am afraid, I put my trust in you. In God, whose word I praise-in God I trust and am not afraid. What can mere mortals do to me?"
—Psalms 56:3-4

_____

_____

Redemptive Grace

_____

_____

"The Lord is with me; I will not be afraid. What can mere mortals do to me?"

—Psalm 118:6

_____

_____

_____

"Say to those with fearful hearts, "Be strong, do not fear; your God will come…"

—Isaiah 35:4

_____

_____

_____

"For I am convinced that neither death nor life, neither angels nor demons, neither the present nor the future, nor any powers, neither height nor depth, nor anything else in all creation, will be able to separate us from the love of God that is in Christ Jesus our Lord."

—Romans 8:38-39

_____

_____

Sickness

_____

_____

_____

_____

_____

_____

_____

Do you see the theme? We are broken humans who are going to hurt. We are going to be in pain. We are going to experience fear. We are going to struggle. Regardless of the obstacle in front of us, if we have chosen to follow God, and if we will allow Him to be loud in our lives, we can run from fear and run to Him! I listed five verses that point to "fear not." The challenge for you is to find five more in the Bible. Write them in the space below. Out of these ten verses, choose at least one to commit to memory. Build up that Scripture arsenal so when the inevitable floods and fires come, you are ready to fight back!

1. _____

_____

2. _____

_____

Redemptive Grace

3. _____

_____

4. _____

_____

5. _____

_____

I commit to memorize:

_____

_____

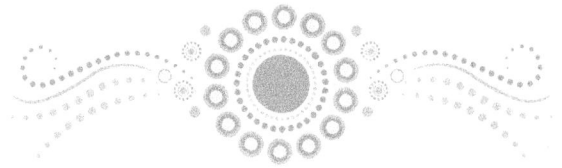

Mama Trauma

"Out of my distress I called on the Lord; the Lord answered me and set me free"

—Psalm 118:5.

My freshman high school English teacher assigned our class a task on the first day of school. We were to write a letter to ourselves to be open our senior year. In that letter, we were to share our hopes, dreams, and goals for the future. We were to include what career we wanted to have, what our personal life would look like, where we would live, etc. I loved that assignment and completed it with no stress at all. I knew my future would involve children. My Mama was a teacher, and I often volunteered in her classroom. I was the eldest of four children, and while we had our ups and downs, for the most part, being a sister was my favorite role in life. I volunteered in the children's ministry at church. I worked in after-school and summer camp programs. I simply loved being around children. In my letter, I wrote that I would be a teacher or counselor and the mom of four children. Those were the ideas I had since I was a little girl and were the dreams that stayed with me into adulthood.

My husband and I were high school sweethearts, and we married when we were nineteen years old. He had joined the Navy. I dropped out of college to go with him on this new adventure. He was my buddy and my caretaker. He had walked through the vocal cord and Crohn's medical issues with me. He had carried me from bed to the bathroom and back again when the flare-ups were debilitating. When he left for the military, it was a no-brainer for me that I would follow him. We were married for a few years when I became pregnant with our first baby. I am a super-nerd and began reading every book on the topic. I checked out birthing videos from the library (a really bad decision in hindsight). I did everything "right." I exercised and I ate well. Thankfully, my Crohn's disease was in remission! With Crohn's if the disease is in remission at conception, it stays in remission the length of the pregnancy ... hallelujah! I played classical music for the baby and read to my growing belly every day. The pregnancy was wonderful. I had a due date for late October, and I was progressing along perfectly.

My sister is awesome and completely different from me. Aside from our core beliefs, she and I are opposites. We balance each other well. When I was expecting my first baby, she was in college and not at all impressed with my condition. My husband and I had moved to southern Georgia in mid-August, and my sister came down during her summer break to help me unpack and set-up the house while my husband drove to the base in Florida every day for work. On August 20, I woke up and started my morning routine. While I was squeezing the toothpaste on my toothbrush, my water broke. I started yelling "this isn't right! It's too early! This isn't what the books said!" I am a type-A, checklist, study hard person; my world was rocked despite me doing everything "right," I was going into labor; plus, my due date was in late

Mama Trauma

October. My sister was not enthused. She would not come into the room, but she did call the ambulance. Fifteen minutes later, a fire truck, an ambulance, and a police car were all in my tiny front yard in front of the house we had lived in for a week. My sister had to call the Red Cross to get an emergency message to my husband. Then, she had to call everyone back home who had a seven-to-eight-hour drive ahead of them to get to us.

I have never been great at math, but even I knew going into labor eight weeks early was not a good thing. The perfect pregnancy had morphed into a traumatic labor. The anesthesiologist who was sent in to start the epidural was brand new and shaking profusely. After three attempts, and a few tears from him, I decided to forego the epidural until I could get a trained doctor. Meanwhile, my husband was in a panic because he also knew the dangers of having a premature baby and struggled seeing me in pain and out of control. After a long day of labor, my little girl was born. When she arrived, the room was silent. She was not breathing. She was blue. She was removed from me and whisked away. There was talk of airlifting her to a children's hospital in Florida. Thankfully, she began to breathe and scream. Her cry was not that of a newborn baby. It was more like the screech of a cat (if you ever watched the Harry Potter films, think of a mandrake). She was finally returned to my arms. Her skin and eyes were yellow with jaundice. She was unable to nurse, so we had to bottle feed her. She was sickly but beautiful. When we were released to go home, we were assigned an in-home nurse who came several times a day to check on our baby. She was placed on a light bed to fight

Redemptive Grace

the jaundice. She had severe colic. She did not sleep. She did not eat well. But she was here; and she was mine! I was finally a mama!

Two and a half years later, I was expecting twins. Unfortunately, this time, my Crohn's Disease was active, which meant it would stay active through the course of the pregnancy. I was very sick during this journey. It was nothing like the first time. I was constantly losing blood. I was having to take vitamin B shots in my lower back a few times a week. Between the swelling from my Crohn's and the growth of two little ones, I blew up pretty quickly. I could not take certain medication while expecting, and I kept getting sicker and sicker. One flare-up landed me in the hospital and during my follow-up visit, I learned I had lost one of the babies. I was devastated; but I had hope. I believe that to be absent from the body is to be in the presence of Jesus—which led me to believe that the baby I lost was with the Creator and that one day I will meet that baby in heaven!

I was placed on bedrest, and there I stayed for the bulk of that pregnancy. Thankfully, we had been able to stay in the same area with the Navy. My husband was out-to-sea a lot, but I had my youngest brother living with me. He and I had a lot of fun nights watching movies and playing games. I was blessed to be involved in an amazing church with an incredibly supportive church family. I had awesome people who helped get me to the doctor, would take care of my toddler, who fixed meals for us, and who prayed for me. What a gift!

Because the books had failed me the first time around, I didn't read them again. And, because my first labor was so long, I figured I had time to take a shower and take my time before going to the hospital when my water broke the second time. Bad call. My husband was home this time, and he rushed me to the hospital where my labor progressed so quickly, the doctor almost didn't arrive in time. There was no time for an epidural. The delivery was easy. No problems. My second little one had arrived, this time a boy! In my head and heart, I had three of my four children. Two on Earth and one in heaven. I was rejoicing in God's goodness.

Two years later, because of a series of life-changing events (which I'll uncover later), my husband and I decided to move back to our hometown. He was out of the Navy at this point, and we felt called to be closer to our aging grandparents and changing family dynamics. One of my friends back home found us a rental house; a friend from the church we had attended in high school promised my husband a job, so we came back in a hurry. When we arrived, the job fell through, and the condition of our families was worse than we realized. My husband looked for work and was able to get a security job that had him working third shift. A lot transpired during this time in my life. I would say it was the darkest part of my history, but we will get to that later. However, a sparkle emerged when I learned I was expecting again. Baby number four! Goal met; checklist complete! I was elated. Being a mom was where I felt life made sense. I was confident in parenting. I loved being home with my children. It was a dream. As we all know, our plans aren't always God's plan. I miscarried that baby.

This time, I was not surrounded by a supportive church family because we had not made connecting to a church a priority. We did have family, but they were dealing with their own crises, and they did all they could in their ability to reach out during this time. We did have some sweet friends who also tried to help. The combination of other things going on in my life with this loss was too much for me. I hit rock bottom.

My security had vanished. My connection to the Lord had been put on hold by me. I could not read my Bible. I could not pray. I was despondent. I would rally for my toddler and preschooler. I would exist around my husband. I would perform when I had to for others. I began to isolate myself. I began to feed lies. I went back to my old mentality of works-based faith. I believed that the loss of another baby was because of my past sin. I believed I was inadequate, unworthy, and a failure. I was defeated by myself. I had given in to lies and darkness. The enemy had full reign in my mind. I didn't even try to combat him.

One night, my husband was at work and both children were asleep in bed. I was overcome by sadness. Every insecurity about myself was playing like a broken medley in my ears. Every failure of my past was showing like a movie in my mind. I was broken. I was giving up. I had a variety of medications on hand from countless hospital visits. I had researched the combination needed to end my life. I was tired. I just wanted to sleep and never wake up. The world would be fine without me. Everyone would cope. It would be fine.

I poured myself a glass of water. I lined up the pills on the counter. I picked them up in my hand, and then the most bizarre and wonderful thing happened to me. I heard a whisper that simply said "stop." That's all. But I heard it. Right beside me, in my right ear. I turned my head to look

Mama Trauma

around, and when I did, I looked straight into my daughter's bedroom. She was sleeping soundly. I was physically alone in that kitchen, but I was not alone spiritually. While I had disconnected from the Lord, He had not disconnected from me. He was with me. In my darkest, most dangerous moment, He was there. He was holding me. He was watching me. He stopped me. I fell onto the kitchen floor and wept. I threw away all the pills. I fell on my face and repented. I gave myself back to God. I confessed my sin of selfishness and allowing fear to control my head and heart. I asked forgiveness for turning my back on God, for believing I wasn't valuable to Him. I called out to Him and asked Him to restore me. It wasn't a magical moment or quick fix. It was the beginning of a process of healing and reconciliation to my Father.

All of us have experienced heartache and loss. We have dealt with dreams that were never to come true. We have faced trials that have laid us flat on our back. In those moments, we must choose. What do we say we believe? Do we actually believe what we say? We have to choose light over darkness. We have to choose truth over lies. We have to dig deeper into the Lord and push farther away from the enemy. But how? It is so daunting.

My first word of advice is to seek help. Find a solid Christian you can talk to. If you don't have a friend or family member that you are comfortable to do this with, seek out a local, Bible-believing, gospel-centered church. They should be able to put you in contact with a pastor or faith-based counselor. Share your burden with them. Ask them to pray with you and for you. If you are in immediate danger, if you are entertaining thoughts of hurting yourself,

Redemptive Grace

PLEASE reach out! There are incredible people who want to walk with you.

Next, I would challenge you to get into the Word. I have been blessed with an awesome counselor who has walked me through many obstacles in my life. His homework assignment that stuck with me the most was to make a list of truths and lies. I am going to pass that assignment on to you. In the space below, make a list of the lies the enemy is telling you.

_____

_____

_____

_____

_____

_____

_____

Now that all of that junk is out of your head and on a piece of paper, let's look at what truths we can find in the Bible. Let's look first about who the enemy is. Read the verses and write out the truth from it:

"The thief comes only to steal and kill and destroy; I [Jesus] have come that they may have life, and have it to the full."
—John 10:10

_____

_____

Mama Trauma

"Be sober-minded; be watchful. Your adversary the devil prowls around like a roaring lion, seeking someone to devour."
—1 Peter 5:8

_____

_____

"For such men are false apostles, deceitful workmen, disguising themselves as apostles of Christ. And no wonder, for even Satan disguises himself as an angel of light."
—2 Corinthians 11:13-14

_____

_____

Get it? Satan wants to win you over. He wants to defeat you. He wants your life for his. When we believe lies, and when we treat his voice as true, we are giving him the victory. BUT GOD IS GREATER! Now, let's look at what the Bible says is true about YOU through the grace of God. Read the scripture and write out the truth from it:

"See what kind of love the Father has given to us, that we should be called children of God; and so we are. The reason why the world does not know us is that they did not know Him."
—1 John 3:1

_____

_____

Redemptive Grace

"But you, O Lord, are a God merciful and gracious, slow to anger and abounding in steadfast love and faithfulness."
—Psalm 86:15

_____

_____

"Give thanks to the God of heaven, for His steadfast love endures forever."
—Psalm 136:26

_____

_____

"Know therefore that the Lord your God is God, the faithful God who keeps covenant and steadfast love with those who love Him and keep His commandments, to a thousand generations…"
—Deuteronomy 7:9

_____

_____

"For God so loved the world, that He gave His only Son, that whoever believes in Him should not perish but have eternal life. For God did not send His Son into the world to condemn the world, but in order that the world might be saved through Him."
—John 3:16-17

_____

_____

Mama Trauma

"But God shows His love for us in that while we were still sinners, Christ died for us."
—Romans 5:8

"As the Father has loved me, so have I loved you. Abide in my love. If you keep my commandments, you will abide in my love, just as I have kept my Father's commandments and abide in His love. These things I have spoken to you, that my joy may be in you, and that your joy may be full. This is my commandment, that you love one another as I have loved you. Greater love has no one than this, that someone lay down his life for his friends. You are my friends if you do what I command you. No longer do I call you servants, for the servant does not know what his master is doing; but I have called you friends, for all that I have heard from my Father I have made known to you. You did not choose me, but I chose you and appointed you that you should go and bear fruit and that your fruit should abide, so whatever you ask the Father in my name, He may give it to you. These things I command you, so that you will love one another."
—John 15:9-17

Redemptive Grace

"No, in all these things we are more than conquerors through Him who loved us. For I am sure that neither death nor life, nor angels nor rulers, nor things present nor things to come, nor powers, nor height no depth, nor anything else is all creation, will be able to separate us from the love of God in Christ Jesus our Lord."

—Romans 8:37-39

_____

_____

"But God, being rich in mercy, because of the great love with which He loved us, even when we were dead in our trespasses, made us alive together with Christ—by grace you have been saved—"

—Ephesians 2:4-5

_____

_____

"For you formed my inward parts; you knitted me together in my mother's womb. I praise you, for I am fearfully and wonderfully made. Wonderful are your works; my soul knows it very well. My frame was not hidden from you, when I was being made in secret, intricately woven in the depths of the earth. Your eyes saw my unformed substance; in your book were written, every one of them, the days that were formed for me, when as yet there was none of them."

—Psalm 139: 13-16

_____

_____

Mama Trauma

"For we are His workmanship, created in Christ Jesus for good works, which God prepared beforehand, that we should walk in them."
—Ephesians 2:10

_____

_____

"So God created man in His own image, in the image of God He created him; male and female He created them."
—Genesis 1:27

_____

_____

Out of all these verses, which one really stood out to you? Which one tugged on your heartstrings as you read it. I encourage you to read all these truths out loud again. Pay attention to which one the Holy Spirit is pointing you towards. Write out that verse below and commit it to memory!

_____

_____

_____

_____

_____

_____

Redemptive Grace

Daddy Issues

"Whatever you do, work heartily as for the Lord and not for men"
—Colossians 3:23

I really did love my childhood. I am the eldest of four children. I love being a big sister. My parents were incredible people. They were hard-working, hospitable, Jesus-loving folks. When I was younger, my Mama worked at the Christian schools we attended. She started in the library then taught PreK. Mama had a gift for teaching. When she was in a classroom of children, she was in her element, and she shone brightly! Mama had the goal of completing her education so she could become an elementary school teacher. When Mama started back to school, I transitioned from the tiny church school to a much larger public middle school. Mama worked at the elementary school where my younger siblings attended. After a full day with lots of kiddos, she would drive to her college classes that were held in the evenings. Mama showed us the importance of setting goals, the sacrifices that have to be made to make some dreams a reality, and the value of an education.

Both of our parents modeled hospitality. Our house was open to anyone, any time. We lived in a very humble home. It wasn't big or fancy, but it was always clean and welcoming. Our Daddy loved people. He could talk to anyone. There were many times people would show up at our house because of a conversation Daddy had with them elsewhere. People of all colors, economic statuses, family structures, and ages would spend time at our house. When Daddy invited people over, Mama would be the ultimate hostess. She would figure out a meal out of whatever ingredients she had on hand. She would make sure the visitors were comfortable. Both of my parents simply loved people well. They didn't have a lot when it came to material possessions, but what they did have, they shared generously with others.

My siblings and I were held to the highest of standards. We were expected to keep our rooms clean. We were taught to do housework and yard work at young ages. We were to be disciplined and obedient. Good grades were a must. Manners were necessary. Bible verses needed to be memorized. When we were in public, we were to remember we represented our family name. I felt a great sense of pressure to be perfect for my siblings. They should have someone positive to look up to. My Daddy would question when my grades would drop from an A to a B, even in honors math where I greatly struggled. In school, I rarely took the easy path. I signed up for every honors or advanced placement course that I could handle. In chorus, if there was a solo open, I would audition. I felt that I constantly was competing with myself to have my parents be proud of me … especially my Daddy.

I have so many great memories of my Daddy and me. I can remember him picking me up from school one birthday and taking me to an ice cream shop … just the two of

Daddy Issues

us, which was extremely rare! I remember playing basketball with him for hours at a time where he would teach me how to shoot and follow-through and where he would always push me to be more aggressive (a quality I greatly lacked). My favorite memories are of the times when we would go to sing somewhere. Daddy would be the person people wanted to hear because of his rich baritone voice and his ability to capture the audience's ear with his story-telling ability. Daddy would take me along to some events and let me sing a song with him. Eventually, I had one or two songs that I would sing on my own in between Daddy's songs. I remember when a sweet man in our church passed away, and his wife asked Daddy and me to sing at the funeral. That is one of the times when I saw my Daddy was truly proud of me. I had been sought out because of my talent; and, he had spent a lot of time and effort honing that talent in me. I don't think my Daddy felt this way, but I transposed the idea into my mind that when I was no longer able to sing, he was no longer proud of me.

Some families shower each other with words of endearment and affection and a million hugs a day; our family wasn't that kind of family. We were the family where we showed each other we loved one another by helping complete chores, cooking a favorite meal, or simply following instructions. Actions showed how we felt. I placed so much weight on approval from my parents, and my heart was set on my Daddy recognizing my achievements. After the aforementioned travesty of confessing my sexual sins to my parents, there was a big change in the dynamic of my relationship with my Daddy. My Mama was more forgiving, but my Daddy took longer to work through things … and that's ok. We all have our processes. In fairness, my Daddy also was at home less and less the older I got. He worked several jobs to provide for our family. There would be the struggle I would face of being upset that I didn't have more time with my Daddy but also not wanting more time because I was convinced I wasn't good enough for him.

After I was married and living away from home, my conversations with my Daddy became fewer. This was before the times of everyone having email or mobile phones. Phone conversations had to be planned, and you had to have the money to pay for a long-distance call. Visits were hard to figure out because of how far away I lived, work schedules, and again, finances. I would get little visits with my Daddy when he would meet me halfway to pick-up my siblings who would come stay with me for some time during the summer and over the Thanksgiving holiday. I am very much to blame for not working harder to maintain a relationship with my Daddy when I moved away.

When my husband would go on deployment, I would come home to visit. I would stay at my Grandmama's house across the road from my parents' home. During one such visit, I noticed some extreme changes in my Daddy's behavior. He was like two different people. He would switch from being a jovial entertainer to an angry screamer. Everyone has stuff. Everyone has issues. We all have personality flaws. This was different. My sister and I participated in a Bible study together, and one of the speaker's gave a testimony that sounded identical to what we were seeing in our Daddy. I prayerfully considered talking to him. When I finally plucked up the courage to ask some difficult questions, the conversation could not have gone more wrong.

Over the course of the next year, many things happened in my family. All the stories are not solely mine to share; and, while I battled with my Daddy, I do not want to paint him as a villain or in an unfair light. By this time, I had an infant daughter. I was concerned by the growing alarming behaviors I would see in my Daddy when I would come home to visit. My husband and I agreed that it was time for me to address some things. I shared my concern with my Daddy. I told him I was worried about him. I implored him to get help. I asked what I could do to help. In my Daddy's eyes, I was completely out of bounds in saying these things. The concerns I had were none of my business. Another string of events happened and the only conversations that were had between my Daddy and me ended with me in tears and him yelling. I didn't know what else to do, and I stopped communicating with him at all. I could not bear the rejection and hurt I felt.

I knew this was not my Daddy. This was a very human man who was hurting. He was constantly under stress. There was never a time in my life where my Daddy was working less than two jobs. There was never a time where he was not trying to care for the people that the rest of society ignores. Daddy was always trying. Life was unbelievably hard. Daddy had personal struggles that he was battling. Those struggles took over his heart and mind. He was a different man.

On Christmas Eve of the year I was carrying my second child and still living far away from home, I received a phone call that my Daddy had died. He had been driving and had either a heart attack or stroke behind the wheel. He had been rushed to the emergency room. He was dead. Our family congregated in our hometown to prepare for the funeral. My Daddy had written my siblings and me Christmas cards. The card to my sister and brothers was full of pride and joy. My card was full of aggression and hurt. I was a disappointment. I had hurt my Daddy. I became extremely angry with him, but there was no time to process anger. My parents had only been divorced a year before this happened so being the eldest sibling, it fell on me to have all the meetings with his jobs and insurance people, to set up payment plans with the hospital, and to strategically plan a funeral that would honor the man whose approval I wanted so desperately but whose last words to me were filled with frustration.

It took me almost two years to work through the hurt and anger I felt. Why would God take my Daddy away before we could repair our relationship? Why wouldn't God rescue Daddy from his struggle? If God knew when my Daddy would die and what he would write to me, why wouldn't He have prompted Daddy to leave me with some kind of word of love?

Here's what I have learned about God. He doesn't always answer my questions, at least not the way I want them answered. What He does do is work through His Word and His people. My Daddy's death occurred only a couple of months after I lost my son's twin. Not too long after his death, my father-in-law also died unexpectedly. Next, I lost my other baby. This was the absolute darkest season of my life to that point.

I know many people who have daddy or mommy "issues." My story is not the only one like that. Here's where I missed

Daddy Issues

the mark as a believer. I was basing my existence on the approval of man. I was obsessed with being good enough for another person. While I do believe in the importance of healthy parent-child relationships, I also know that every parent and every child is flawed and filled with sin. Apart from God, how can two sinful people interact in spite of their shortcomings to a positive place? Neither my Daddy nor I were using Jesus as the mediator in our relationship. I justified my decision to cut him out of my life because he would not make changes. Oh, how I missed the understanding of what grace is. I had no concept of mercy. All I had was self-righteousness, judgement, and pride.

Regardless of what our sin struggle is, Jesus paid the price for it … completely … once and for all. When we take that step of faith, when we acknowledge our sins, and when we ask for His forgiveness, we are covered! We shouldn't use that great gift as an excuse to keep wallowing in our sin. Instead, we should feel so thankful for what Jesus did that that same love should spill out of us and into the lives of others. That doesn't just happen. It takes some training.

Think to a time when you sought the approval of another. What were you hoping to experience? What did you "do" to try and gain those desired accolades?

_____

_____

_____

_____

Redemptive Grace

Can you think of a time when someone sought approval from you? How did you react? What were your thoughts?

_____

_____

_____

_____

Now, think of a time when you showed judgement to another person. Did you feel justified in your thoughts and behaviors? Did you feel regret or remorse?

_____

_____

_____

Let's change gears. I have heard many pastors and teachers explain what grace is by using the acronym God's Riches At Christ's Expense. Translation? Grace is the gift of Jesus' life in exchange for the cost of our sin. There is nothing we could do to earn grace. Likewise, mercy is a gift. Mercy is the act of forgiving wrongdoing when a punishment is owed. Can you think of a time when you were shown grace? Mercy? What was the situation? What was the end result? How did you feel?

_____

_____

_____

Daddy Issues

Finally, think of a time when you were given the opportunity to extend grace and mercy to another person. Were you able to? Was it an easy decision or action? How did the situation play out? How did you feel after being gracious or merciful?

_____

_____

_____

_____

Let's look at Scripture. The Bible is full of verses that speak to the struggle of approval of man and the consequences of falling prey to that. Thankfully, the Bible also gives us plenty of guidance on how to reconfigure our mindset to look to our Creator for our identity. Read these verses and underline the similarities; take note of the theme!

"The fear of man lays a snare, but whoever trusts in the Lord is safe."
—Proverbs 29:25

_____

_____

"Stop regarding a man in whose nostrils is breath, for what account is he?"
—Isaiah 2:22

_____

_____

Redemptive Grace

"For am I now seeking the approval of man, or of God? Or am I trying to please man? If I were still trying to please man, I would not be a servant of Christ."

—Galatians 1:10

"Whatever you do, work heartily, as for the Lord and not for men ..."

—Colossians 3:23

"But just as we have been approved by God to be entrusted with the gospel, so we speak, not to please man, but to please God who tests our hearts."

—1 Thessalonians 2:4

"For they loved the glory that comes from man more than the glory that comes from God."

—John 12:43

Daddy Issues

"How can you say to your brother, 'Brother, let me take out the speck that is in your eye,' when you yourself do not see the log that is in your own eye? You hypocrite, first take the log out of your own eye, and then you will see clearly to take out the speck that is in your brother's eye."

—Luke 6:42

_____

_____

_____

"but God shows His love for us in that while we were still sinners, Christ died for us."

—Romans 5:8

_____

_____

_____

I think the last verse is the perfect one to end this section. "While we were still sinners," which is an ongoing human condition, "Christ died for us." While we were stuck in sin, are actively battling sin, or are prepping for our next sin, Christ still died for us. He knew our most disgusting, ugliest, scariest selves and yet, He still gave up His life for us. Isn't that amazing? Now, the challenge is to look at others through that same lens. What Jesus did for you, He did for every human! What a powerful and humbling thought!

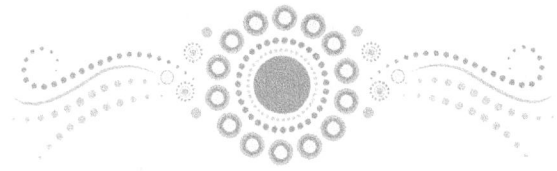

Details

"... Consider the lilies of the field, how they grow: they neither toil nor spin, yet I tell you, even Solomon in all his glory was not arrayed like one of these. But if God so clothes the grass of the field, which today is alive and tomorrow is thrown into the oven, will He so much more clothe you, O you of little faith?"

—Matthew 6:28-30

My Grandmama was a seamstress. She was incredibly gifted. Sure, she could hem pants, repair a zipper, and even make a "hippie" dress if I asked for it. Beyond that, Grandmama had a special skill set. As far back as I can remember, Grandmama worked in a bridal salon. I used to love going to work with her on Saturdays. She would allow my sister and me to help hang up dresses and style mannequins. We would make signs to hang up on the sale rack. We would straighten up the magazine area and vacuum the carpet. She would take us to Burger King for lunch and give us money to get candy from the drug store next door. If there was a slow day, Grandmama would even let me try on dresses! While I wouldn't say that I was a girly-girl growing up, I did appreciate pretty things. There was this one dress that I coveted. The bodice of the dress was gold with jewels lining the top. The skirt was yards and yards of white tulle with gold flecks. When I saw that dress, I was inspired. When I would try on the dress, I would feel elegant and important. Apparently, I was the only person in our town who loved that gown. For years it hung on the sales rack. Every time I visited the shop, I would run the material through my fingers. I cannot imagine how many times Grandmama helped in and out of the dress. Then, my senior year of high school, the gold dress became mine! I graced the stage of my high school's musical wearing the gown I had been drawn to since I was a little girl.

Grandmama always had a sewing room wherever she lived. The room would be filled with ball gowns, bridesmaid attire, prom dresses and bridal ensembles. Her sewing room was a showroom. She was known in our community for her talent and local celebrities visited her home from time to time to have their dresses altered just right. The sewing room had two machines set on top of sturdy tables. In one corner of the room was a cabinet of drawers filled with sequins, pearls, lace, tulle, and all things that sparkled. There was a smaller cabinet stuffed with thread of various colors and strengths. On one wall was an ingenious creation of Grandmama's design ... a small platform with a yard stick attached in order so she could measure each hemline perfectly. On another wall was a floor length mirror where the patron could take in the beauty of her gown and watch Grandmama painstakingly measure and pin. Every girl who entered that room was treated as if she was the first girl to ever go to a dance, the first bride to walk down an aisle.

I was so blessed to have a personal seamstress. Not only was my Grandmama skilled with the needle and thread, but

Details

she was also the most frugal person. Every homecoming or prom dress I had was found at a steal of a deal. Truly, my senior prom dress was nineteen dollars! We would look for dresses where the price was right, then Grandmama would make the dress fit me, as if it were designed specifically for me. Grandmama was not a talkative person. She was no-nonsense. I was most scolded by her for being "foolish"… translation, I was perky, chatty, and sang a lot of the time. Our personalities were not the same, but we worked well together. I remember one time we were searching for a homecoming dress at the mall, and while I was trying them on, my Grandmama told me, "Amber, you'll be a great mother." I almost passed out! She did not give out compliments. I was blushing with pride when the sentence continued. "You've got big hips that will make it easy to carry a baby." There you go. Thanks, Grandmama.

When I was in college, I was invited to the spring formal, and I wanted a dress from my Grandmama. She and I went fabric shopping, and I picked out the prettiest print of dark green and blue. I had it measured and cut and felt that I was doing my Grandmama proud. I picked out a pattern, and we headed to her house. A few weeks later, when the dress was completed, I tried it on and felt lovely. My Grandmama said it was the ugliest dress with the "loudest" fabric she had ever made. She then asked if I was sure I wanted to wear it in public. It's still one of my favorite things I have ever worn.

There was a sweet side to my Grandmama, too. When I decided to drop out of college, get married, and move away from home when I was nineteen years old, my Grandmama was one of my biggest supporters and helpers. I doubt that she agreed with my choice, but she helped me, nonetheless. She took my Mama, sister, and me to a wholesale warehouse where we purchased all the flowers. She designed and made the bouquets and boutonnieres. She scouted our town for the best prices for suits for the men and boys. She made my wedding dress.

Now, to work in a bridal salon for years and years, to know every designer's name, to know the price points and the styles put my Grandmama ahead of the game when it came to wedding dress searching. The hunting party for the perfect dress included my Mama, my sister and my Grandmama. My Mama was a mess because I was getting married and leaving. To her, I looked perfect in everything. My sister was unimpressed by gowns and thought I was crazy for getting married. My Grandmama was the voice of truth. We went all over the place looking for the dress that was in my head. I could never find "the one"; at least not "the one" for "the price." It didn't help that I was getting married in the winter but had always wanted a summer, outdoor wedding.

One day, I was at the mall looking for bridesmaid dresses, and I saw a simple white corset-style bodice hanging randomly in the dress section. I bought it and took it to my Grandmama. My fingers were crossed that I had made a smart purchase and that Grandmama would approve. Grandmama took the bodice in her hand, turned it over a few times, examined the seams, traced the lines with her finger, tested the zipper, then looked at me. "It's plain. It's not you. But I can make it yours."

Details

Over the next few weeks, Grandmama would work on my dress. The skirt was simple, yet lovely. The bustle was small, but feminine. Grandmama had to make alterations to that gown repeatedly before the wedding because of health problems I was having. I was losing weight at a scary pace, and she never complained when I would try it on, and she would have to take it in and adjust. What I remember the most, what drew me in was the transformation to the corset. For most of her work, Grandmama would use a sewing machine. But, for the intricate details, she would get out her needle and thread.

I would sit on the couch beside her for hours with home and garden shows playing in the background. I would watch her keen and nimble fingers weave the perfect design of gems around the edges of the bodice. She would attach a single pearl at a time. The work was tedious. It was mesmerizing. It was rigorous. And it was beautiful. The thread is what held every seam in place from every alteration, what attached every sparkle to the fabric and helped it to shimmer in the light, and what transformed something simple into something stunning.

My Grandmama taught me many things, but I did not inherit her gift for working with thread and fabric. Every dress she took into her sewing room was given the most intensive attention. The ladies who would come to pick up their gowns would oooh and ahhh over the end result. Grandmama would point out every stitch, sequin and change that was made to specifically showcase the beauty of the girl wearing the dress.

When God created each one of us, He did so with intensity and intentionality. Every innate gift or skill we have was placed into our genetic makeup by the Creator of the Universe. Your personality, your talents, your strengths, your weaknesses are all part of your beautifully unique design. The same way my Grandmama painstakingly transformed a simple bodice into a work of wearable art, God put together the pieces of your existence. There are debates in the church concerning predestination and free will, and I'm not going to take that topic on in-depth here. I am going to say that God has a plan. He has a will for our lives. He has given us an example to live by through His Son, Jesus. He has given us a helper on earth in the Holy Spirit. He has given us an open line of communication to Him through prayer. He has given us a guidebook to making decisions in life with His Word, the Bible. He has greatly equipped us to take on the challenges of life. I don't visualize God as a puppet master shuffling us down the roads of life. I see Him as a loving father who has given His children opportunities to choose to follow Him, to choose to make God-honoring choices, to choose to strive for a life set apart from the rest of the world.

I write all of this to remind you that you are a valuable part of creation. You are a puzzle piece in the grand puzzle of the universe. You are a beloved, special, hand-made, original portrait of art made by the ultimate artist. Life wears us down. The world beats these truths out of our minds. Our life choices often divvy out consequences that cause us to doubt our worth. The enemy would love to win each one of us over by stacking lies up in our mind. How do we combat those falsehoods? We fight with the sword of the Spirit!

Details

Let's prepare for those inevitable battles now. Read the following Scriptures then rewrite them in a personal way. What do these verses say about you or to you? Use personal pronouns or even your name. Remember, the Bible is God's living, breathing words spoken to each one of us!

Example:
"'For I know the plans I have for you,' declares the Lord, 'plans to prosper you and not to harm you, plans to give you hope and a future.'"

—Jeremiah 29:11

"'Even if I don't see the plan, I know God has made plans just for me. His plans are to be helpful to me and not to hurt me. He plans to give me hope and a future.'"

—Jeremiah 29:11

"I know that you can do all things; no purpose of yours can be thwarted [opposed] …"

—Job 42:2

_____

_____

_____

"Your Word is a lamp for my feet, and a light on my path."
—Psalm 119:105

_____

_____

Redemptive Grace

"The Lord will fulfill His purpose for me; your steadfast love, O Lord, endures forever ..."

—Psalm 138:8

"In their hearts humans plan their course, but the Lord establishes their steps."

—Proverbs 16:9

"For God so loved the world that He gave His one and only Son, that whoever believes in Him shall not perish but have eternal life. For God did not send His Son into the world to condemn the world, but to save the world through Him." (Fill your name in instead of 'world').

—John 3:16-17

"But the Advocate, the Holy Spirit, whom the Father will send in my name, will teach you all things and will remind you of everything I have said to you."

—John 14:26

Details

"But God demonstrates His own love for us in this: while we were still sinners, Christ died for us."
—Romans 5:8

"And we know that in all things God works for the good of those who love Him, who have been called according to His purpose."
—Romans 8:28

"For it is by grace you have been saved, through faith—and this is not from yourselves, it is the gift of God—not by works, so that no one can boast. For we are God's handiwork, created in Christ Jesus to do good works, which God prepared in advance for us to do."
—Ephesians 2:8-10

Redemptive Grace

"... being confident of this, that He who began a good work in you will carry it on to completion until the day of Christ Jesus."

—Philippians 1:6

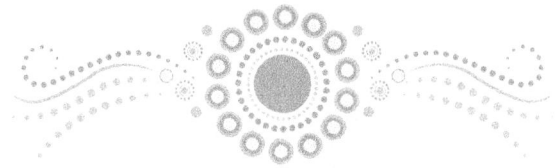

Hard Work

"Whatever you do, work at it with all your heart, as working for the Lord, not for men ..."
—Colossians 3:23

I was incredibly fortunate to grow up in a family where a hard work ethic was daily modeled for me. My parents married young and started their family together a couple of years into marriage. In their younger days, college was not an option for every teenager who graduated high school. Both of my parents began working while students and continued working as they grew their family. My Daddy had a manufacturing job, and my Mama ran an in-home daycare when I was born. As my siblings came along, my Mama stayed home to take care of us. My youngest brother was born with a myriad of medical issues, and the medical expenses piled up quickly. My Daddy started working a second job at the local grocery store bagging groceries. As soon as my youngest brother reached preschool age, my Mama found a Christian school where all four of us could attend for free while she worked as a librarian and preschool assistant.

I attended the small, sweet, sheltered Christian school during my elementary school years. The summer before I started 6th grade, my Mama took a job as a reading teacher assistant for a public elementary school. My siblings went to the school where she worked, and I started my public-school career in middle school (but that's a whole other story!). While she started this new job, Mama also started going to college at night to earn her education degree. She graduated from college one week before I graduated high school! Talk about commitment! At the same time, my Daddy was working at least two jobs. As technology advanced, he was laid off. He had earned an associate's degree from the local community college, but the degree aligned with machine work, and it was incredibly difficult for him to find a new career that held the same income and benefits. Daddy would work two to three jobs to support our family.

During this time, our family faced many medical trials. My youngest brother continued to have appointments at children's hospitals out-of-state. My Mama had a series of medical complications. My sister and I both contracted mononucleosis from a mission trip. My other brother was a walking accident-attracting-tornado. This is also the time all my other medical issues came to light. There was no letup in doctor appointments. There was no grace for medical bills. As an adult, I know the expenses we have in our little family, and I cannot fathom the choices and sacrifices my parents had to make concerning our world.

When I look back at my childhood, I have so many happy memories. We didn't travel or take big vacations. We would visit friends and family who lived in cities within driving distance to have a change of scenery. We rarely ate out at restaurants, and when we did, there was usually a celebratory

Hard Work

reason. We didn't typically have new clothes, but my Mama was a bargain-shopper and could find great deals when we outgrew our clothes. She and my Grandmama were expert yard-salers and consignment-shoppers. We also had many hand-me-downs. I remember seasons where we had food stamps and when we would visit a food pantry. I had no idea what our financial situation was as a child. Because my parents took such good care of us, I never realized we were growing up right on the poverty line.

When my Mama started back to college and my Daddy was working his various jobs, my Grandmama built a house across the road from ours. This way, she could help take care of us. Until I became a licensed driver, Grandmama would pick us up from school, take us to sports practices or drop us off at church. She would cook dinner. She would make sure we had baths and went to bed at the appropriate time. Grandmama would also keep some treats on hand for us and every once in a while, she would take us to the local discount bakery to pick out something sugary.

It was important to my parents and Grandmama that my siblings and I understood the value of an education. The standards set for us in school were very high. We were expected to make good grades, and if we struggled in a subject, they would find someone to help us over that academic hurdle. In athletics, we were to be respectful of our coaches and were commanded to always give our best efforts. In chorus and drama, we were challenged to audition for parts and to sing at church and school. The only thing my siblings and I collectively bucked on was piano. The sweet and extremely patient pianist from our church gave us piano lessons, and it was the only activity that all four of us rebelled on. However, we are all thankful that we can read music because of that training!

My siblings and I also were equipped in house and yard work. When Daddy was home, he taught us how to mow lawns and wash cars. Mama showed us how to do laundry, clean house, and keep everything organized. Grandmama made sure we knew a flower from a weed, how to operate all the lawn equipment, and how to maintain cars. We didn't grow up in a work camp. The adults made sure we had lots of fun! But the fun didn't happen until the chores were done. During the times when we were with Grandmama, she taught me how to cook southern comfort food. As the four of us grew older, and I took on the responsibility of driving everyone everywhere, I felt secure in knowing what was expected for me. When I left home at nineteen to move a thousand miles from home with my new husband, I felt confident in how to take care of a home!

While it was a daily part of our family fabric to be at work, the work didn't stop at our house. My parents did not have a lot of free time. However, when they were not working, we were usually at church, or we were at someone else's house visiting or helping them out. My parents and Grandmama would take us to visit older people. When we would go into a house, we would start with sharing Bible verses that we had memorized or singing a hymn. Then, we often took on a project. I remember several occasions of loading cleaning or yard work supplies into my Grandmama's car and going to one of her "elderly" friend's house to clean. We would spend hours doing anything from pulling weeds to taking down wallpaper to moving furniture

Hard Work

to waxing floors. Truly, one of my proudest moments was when my Grandmama, who gave compliments sparingly, told one of her friends to allow me to clean her bathroom because "that girl can really clean a tub and toilet." High praise!

Having a strong work ethic is an integral part of who I am. When I see something that someone needs, I want to do it. When I have an idea in my head for a project, I want to knock it out. Being someone committed to hard work is admirable. Maybe you are all in for your career, your education, your family, your creative outlet, your favorite volunteer organization. Do you apply that same work ethic into your spiritual walk? I can spend 30 minutes cleaning a bathroom floor or a whole day sorting apples at a food bank. However, I can also sit down to read my Bible or pray, and I'm watching the clock to get to my next task. Do you ever do that? How can we apply that same can-do attitude to our spiritual growth? First, let's look at what Proverbs says about work.

"Whoever works his land will have plenty of bread, but he who follows worthless pursuits lacks sense."
—Proverbs 12:11

"The hand of the diligent will rule, while the slothful will be put to forced labor."
—Proverbs 12:24

"The soul of the sluggard craves and gets nothing, while the soul of the diligent is richly supplied."
—Proverbs 13:4

Redemptive Grace

"In all toil there is profit, but mere talk tends only to poverty."
—Proverbs 14:23

"Commit your work to the Lord, and your plans will be established."
—Proverbs 16:3

I love Proverbs. It's a book of one-liners that sound commonsensical when you first read them, but when you let the words simmer, you realize they pack a punch. If I were to sum up these five Proverbs, the message would be—be lazy, get nothing; put in the work for the Lord, and He'll provide. When I read these Proverbs, I think "of course I'll work hard. That's why I stay busy!" I am missing the point. I have to apply that same 'let's do this' mentality about my spiritual work.

So, let's figure out how we can transform our minds and habits to give the work that really matters the attention it deserves. Hear my heart, I don't have a foolproof formula, and I still drop the ball when it comes to spiritual discipline; but, when I have a plan of action, I am more likely to be successful! Feel free to use these ideas in your life. Tweak the plan to work for your lifestyle. Add things I didn't think of. Just get movin!'

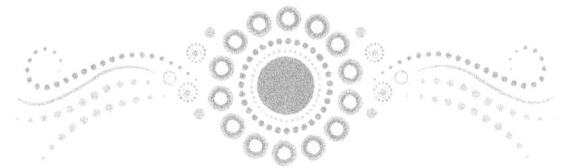

Spiritual Discipline Work Plan

- **Choose a time to designate as your spiritual work out time.** My career requires me to be up and functioning early in the morning before the rest of my household is awake. I have found it is easier for me to wake up 30 minutes earlier in the morning. The house is quiet, there are no distractions. I program my coffee pot the night before, so I grab my cup of coffee, go to my desk, take a deep breath, and get going.

_____

_____

_____

_____

- **Use what you like.** Some people use a notebook and pen. Some people use their laptop, phone, or tablet. Some people use a Bible application, others use the Bible they've had since high school. It doesn't matter what kind of person you are. Use what you know. Use what you like. Every time you sit down, have your Bible and a way to take notes. Read His Word. Write down or type up

Redemptive Grace

your thoughts, questions, and whatever else God places on your heart during that time.

___

___

___

___

- **Have an accountability partner.** Enlist the help of a close, trusted friend who will check in on you. Allow this person to ask you tough questions. Be honest. Tell your friend when you don't complete your work for the day. Let them know when you reach a milestone. Take it up a notch and do a Bible study or have a prayer time with your accountability partner. Pray for God to show you who this person could be in your life. Write their name here!

___

___

___

___

- **Have a study plan.** There are times when I like to make my own study. I like to pick a topic and research it in the Bible. I really enjoy doing a word study. Recently, I took on the task of finding out what the Bible says about "joy," and I was overwhelmed with so many times of being up-

Spiritual Discipline Work Plan

lifted in my quiet time. We live in a time where there are so many excellent sources to help you start a study regime. There are excellent authors and even applications that can assist you get into a rhythm. Don't be afraid if you start a study and you don't finish it. There are a few authors I tried and just couldn't compute their information, or I had an unsettled feeling in my stomach, so I discontinued reading their work. If there is an author you like, read everything they've written. Ask your friends or call a local church and ask for recommendations (just make sure the church is a Gospel-centered, Jesus-centered church). Even better, open up your Bible and get started. I have a study Bible that has changed the way I read the Bible. At the bottom of each page, there is additional information or explanations to help any reader understand the content. I would recommend starting in the Gospels (Matthew, Mark, Luke, John) and read about the life of Jesus. Reading the book of Psalms is also very user-friendly and inspiring! I fully believe that if you make the effort and are reading God's words, He will bless you and open the eyes of your heart to take in what you're reading.

_____

_____

_____

_____

- **Join a Bible study group.** If you attend church, find out what Bible study groups are available. Small group study

Redemptive Grace

is so beneficial. In these environments, we can gain perspective from others, ask questions, share struggles, and have built-in accountability.

_____

_____

_____

_____

- **Be an active part of a Gospel-centered, Jesus-following church congregation.** The Christian life was not meant to be lived alone. Joining a church allows you to be under Biblical teaching and corporate worship. It also can connect you to small groups within the church of like-minded people who are taking on the same challenge of life that you are. Having a church family offers support, training, and a place to use your unique skill set to help others and to glorify God!

_____

_____

_____

_____

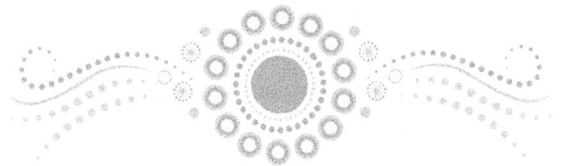

These Three Remain

"And now these three remain: faith, hope and love…"
—I Corinthians 13:13a.

    Thus far, I have shared the struggles in my life and challenged you to take on the obstacles from your life. Let's take some time for some refreshment. While my stories are etched in pain, there were always constant "behind the scenes" people praying for my family and me. These incredible people made deep impacts on my life. They were not my physical flesh and blood, but they were those who were in my life from day one. They are still very much a part of my life. While one has passed away, the other three are still here; and I know no matter what, I could call them with any burden, and they would pray for me and with me. They are my spiritual role models. When I read the above passage today, "these three remain: faith, hope and love," the names of these powerhouse individuals were brought quickly to my mind.

    My "Aunt" Martha is a faith hero. She was my godmother growing up. She was around from the day I was born. She still checks in on me amid the adventures of her life. She is the largest person of faith whom I know. She has the sweetest disposition, a sharp wit, and a fantastic way with words. I have bountiful memories of time with my sweet Aunt Martha. I remember when I was in seventh grade and had written a speech for English class that my teacher had submitted into a contest. There was an opportunity to attend an event to give the speech and the chance to win an award. My Mama went to school at night, my Daddy worked nights, and my Grandmama was taking care of my siblings (who would be less than thrilled to attend a night of middle school speech-giving). My Aunt Martha was the one who took me. She picked me up, took me to dinner, and she and I headed to the event. I remember when I stood up to share my speech feeling confident because Aunt Martha was there. I knew she was praying for me as I spoke. That night I won second place. I remember feeling the combination of pride and disappointment. More than that, I remember Aunt Martha hugging me and telling me that God was going to use me and my words. As I have grown up and gone through many trials, Aunt Martha is the one I know I can email with all the details. I know she will pray over me and the situation. I know she will point out God's truth through it all. I know she will remind me that God is sovereign. She has faced her own trials through life, and through them all, she gives God the glory. Her faith never seems to waiver.

There is a couple in my life who radiate with hope. My "Uncle" Chip and "Aunt" Denise always seem to remember that no matter the circumstance, God is going to show up and show out. These two rock stars were also around at the start of my life. I can remember countless parties, dinners, and visits with them. I remember time spent in their home (which was basically where we went on our family vacations. They were always so hospitable). I can remember my Uncle Chip helping me learn to drive. I can remember my Aunt Denise helping my Mama make sure I had the best baby showers. I remember when I faced medical trials, Uncle Chip would joke with me, and Aunt Denise would feel certain God would bring answers. When I went through my divorce, they both reached out to me and my ex-husband (more on all of that coming up soon). They prayed fervently for reconciliation. They had hope that our family could be saved. When they learned the circumstances that would prevent reconciliation, they began to hope and pray for whatever and whoever God had next for me. I remember sitting in the parking lot of a Firehouse Subs a few years ago and having my Uncle Chip pray over the phone for me, knowing my Aunt Denise was sitting beside him praying quietly. Anytime they are in town, we get together. When I am with them, my hope is recharged. When I get a text or email checking on my family and me, I am encouraged. They never act defeated. They never allowed me to have an attitude of giving up. They shared their hope with me; and they continue to lift me up!

When I think of love, I know I was blessed to have had many years with the personification of love in my dear "Aunt" Rose. Aunt Rose passed away several years ago. I miss her greatly. I still have her phone number embedded in my brain, and there are times when I just want to call her and hear her charming southern drawl. Aunt Rose oozed love. She hugged me as soon as I walked through the door. If I sat beside her, she would hold my hand or pat my arm as we talked. When we were younger, my brothers, sister and myself looked forward to the days when we knew we were making the drive to her house on the other side of town. We always had fun running around the yard, walking to the creek, picking tomatoes in the garden, or climbing the perfect tree in the front yard. The highlight of any visit was when Aunt Rose would call us into the kitchen to give us whatever delectable delight she had baked. Everything in her kitchen was made from scratch. Her red velvet cake would melt the instant it touched the tongue. Her Christmas fudge was so good that one piece was never enough. While we would be in the kitchen, Aunt Rose would ask us to share what Bible verse we were learning, to sing a hymn, or to share a Bible story. She always had a smile on her face ... always. She knew the favorite dessert of everyone in our family, and she would make that dessert for our birthdays. When my Daddy passed away, I lived seven hours away from family and friends, and I struggled deeply with anger. I would call Aunt Rose and she would speak Scripture to me. Her tone was like music. No matter what she said, her words were sweet like honey. I remember her telling me that holding onto anger would damage my heart and eventually my testimony. Those words stung because they were true; but they also began a wonderful healing process. Aunt Rose went through an intense amount of physical pain, especially towards the end of her life. She never complained of hurting. When I lived far away, I always wanted to be able to hop into the car and go see her. Her words were so wise and so loving. Whenever I think of a spiritual role model, she fits the bill. She exemplified the love of Christ in the way she loved others.

    Let's get to work! Read this passage three times. First, just read. Second, go through and underline what love is and what love is not. Finally, when you get to the bold print, write your name over the word love. Now, read the passage again, out loud, saying your name where the word love is.

These Three Remain

"If I speak in the tongues of men and angels, but have not love, I am a noisy gong or a clanging cymbal. And if I have prophetic powers, and understand all mysteries and all knowledge, and if I have all faith, so as to remove mountains, but have not love, I am nothing. If I give away all I have, and if I deliver up my body to be burned, but have not love, I gain nothing.

Love is patient and kind; love does not envy or boast; it is not arrogant or rude. It does not insist on its own way; it is not irritable or resentful; it does not rejoice at wrongdoing but rejoices with the truth.

Love bears all things, believes all things, hopes all things, endures all things.

Love never ends ...

So now these three remain: faith, hope and love; but the greatest of these is love."

—I Corinthians 13:1-8, 13

How did that feel? How did you match up to the Scripture? While I know I will never be perfect, I do accept the challenge of being a Christ follower to try and live a holy life. Holy can be a scary word, but it simply means to be set apart.

Redemptive Grace

The Bible gives us so many examples to help us learn how to strive towards holiness. Inserting your name throughout this passage is an exercise not to make you feel inadequate but to remind you that as a son or daughter of God, you have the Holy Spirit residing within you, and you have the quest to be holy in your heart. This exercise is to help you focus on the truth of what love is and to check where your heart and mind are on that path to being as much like Jesus as you can.

I Corinthians 13 is a Scripture passage that many of us may know from attending weddings. This chapter is often referred to as the "love chapter" in the Bible. It truly is a beautiful piece to read, full of truth, encouragement, conviction, and challenge. I have read this part of the Bible over and over and over. I have read it through the romantic perspective … how do I shape up as a wife when it comes to all these attributes? I have read it through the eyes of family … how am I using the passage to determine how I am being love to my children, parents, and siblings? More importantly, I need to read it through the eyes of someone who wants to show Jesus to a dark and dying world. God is love. Jesus lived a life of love. We are called to love.

How about you? Think back over your life. Who are the spiritual role models you have had? How have they impacted your life? Write down those names and how they have walked with you on your spiritual journey. Want some non-existent extra credit from me? Send them a text, email, or snail mail to let them know what they've done for you!

_____

_____

These Three Remain

_____

_____

Maybe you are someone who did not grow up with spiritual mentors. Maybe you have come to faith by your own research and putting yourself out there. If so, that's amazing! You can still work through this. What impact do you want to have on others? What kind of role model do you want to be? We all have people looking to us every day. Like it or not, we are modeling something for everyone. It can be daunting to think about being a spiritual role model for others. Do not be overwhelmed or intimidated! Let's break down I Corinthians 13 for some pointers.

"If I speak in the tongues of men and of angels, but have not love, I am a noisy gong or a clanging cymbal."

—13:1

Are you someone who talks a lot? Do you speak eloquently? That's fine; but, without love, those words are just noise! Make your words count. When you speak, be someone whose words are backed with love. Give an example of how you can put this into action.

_____

_____

_____

_____

Redemptive Grace

"If I have prophetic powers, and understand all mysteries and all knowledge, and if I have all faith, so as to remove mountains, but have not love, I am nothing."

—13:2

Are you a smart guy or gal? Do you have the answer to almost every question? Are you someone who has bold faith? All of those are great! Again, without love, those qualities mean nothing. Think of a time when you were on the receiving end of getting an answer without love. What happened? How did it make you feel? How would you have responded if the answer had been given with some love?

_____

_____

_____

"If I give away all I have and if I deliver my body to be burned, but have not love, I gain nothing."

—13:3

This verse makes me think of my friends who don't know Jesus but who are self-confessed "good people." They do all the right things. They give to the poor, they volunteer their time, they support all the causes. While all the boxes are being checked off as good works, the actions are empty because the love of God is missing. Have you ever been trapped in that mentality? I know I have. This is definitely the verse that deserves my attention. If I'm helping, I better check my heart

These Three Remain

first—am I helping to do what's right, or am I giving because God gave to me? Think of a time when you have been caught up in doing good, but where you may have been missing the heartbeat behind the work.

_____

_____

_____

_____

_____

"Love is patient and kind; love does not envy or boast; it is not arrogant or rude. It does not insist on its own way; it is not irritable or resentful."

—13:4

This verse is an easy one to read, but it's a challenging one to digest. So ... are you? Are you patient and kind? Are you envious, boastful, arrogant, or rude? Is it your way or the highway? Are you irritable or resentful? Jot down the areas from this verse that you know you can work on.

_____

_____

_____

_____

_____

Redemptive Grace

"It does not rejoice in wrongdoing but rejoices with the truth."

—13:6

Another simple verse here. Are you glad when you pull off something wrong or when something wrong happens to someone else? Do you celebrate when the truth wins out, even if it's not what you wanted? What could be a challenge in shifting your mindset to rejoice in truth?

_____

_____

_____

"Love bears all things, believes all things, hopes all things, endures all things."

—13:7

This poetic verse is the one that packs a punch for me. The Message Bible says it like this: "*[Love] puts up with anything, trusts God always, always looks for the best, never looks back.*" Whoa. That's a lot for my brain to process. Isn't it funny how the simple things can often be the most challenging? I am definitely not a person who has embraced this verse yet, but I am actively working on having this verse be in my heart. My first step is to memorize it. Secondly, I'm going to write it somewhere that I can see it everyday. Finally, I am going to take note of the opportunities God places in my life to live it how. How about you? What are

These Three Remain

you going to do to take this small verse and make it primary in your world?

_____

_____

_____

"Love never ends…"

—13:8

Isn't that beautiful? Love never ends. It doesn't fail. It doesn't quit. Rest in that. No matter what comes your way, God's love is unstoppable! Think back of a time when you felt abandoned or forgotten… maybe a broken relationship, a lost job, a prodigal child, BUT you felt God's presence in your life. Thank Him for that and look expectantly for Him to keep showing up in your world with lots of love!

_____

_____

_____

"So now faith, hope, and love remain; but the greatest of these is love."

—13:13

The motivation for this chapter for me was because of the spiritual mentors in my life who showcased faith, hope and love to me. They have helped me grow into the person I

Redemptive Grace

am. Now, I want to be a person of faith, hope and love. I want to help others experience the benefits of living a life where those attributes trump everything else. So, let's keep working together!

_____

_____

_____

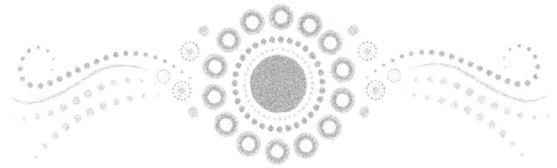

Brotherly (and Sisterly) Love

"Above all, love each other deeply, because love covers a multitude of sins."

—1 Peter 4:8

As I've mentioned several times, I am the eldest of four children. Two years after I was born came my sister, Andrea; two years later, my brother Tyler arrived; and, two years after that, my baby brother, Timothy, rounded out our crew. We lived in a small but warm house. We didn't have a lot in the way of money and things, but we had so much in the ways of love, creativity, and adventures. It is safe for me to assume that if you asked any of my siblings their thoughts on our childhood, they would have positive things to share. Our age range gave us built in companions, playmates, and sometimes subjects to torture.

God is so creative, and one of my favorite ways to observe and study His ability to defy science is to look at families. In our family, we had four children from the same father and mother who shared a genetic code but who were vastly different from each other. I love that. I love that God can take the materials of life and shape such unique creations. While there were many qualities all four of us had, our personalities, thought processes, gift sets, and actions were quite diverse. I've shared a lot about how I'm wired—type-A, perfectionist, approval-seeking, theatrical, and emotional. My incredible sister, Andrea, likes things a certain way and keeps things in order. She is also a deep thinker. She would rather avoid the spotlight, but she will do everything in her power to make sure the person in the light is well-prepared. Andrea is artistic and a problem-solver. She is without a doubt the most resolved person I know. My brother, Tyler, is a performer. He is at ease in a room with 5 people and is right at home on a stage in front of hundreds. He is charismatic, charming, and has just enough self-deprecating humor to make people laugh without making them feel pity for him. Tyler is a champion for what he believes, and he is loyal to a fault. Like Tyler, Timothy is unbelievably loyal to those he loves. He, too, is comfortable in front of an audience, but he is more pensive. When he acts or sings, he is wanting to make the viewer think something. Timothy has a great, biting sense of humor. He cares very deeply, and he stands firm on what he thinks. So, we have some similar traits, but without a doubt, our delivery on our traits can be extremely versatile.

Growing up surrounded by others absolutely shaped me. Even now, I hate to have a quiet house; I would much rather have people all over the place talking and laughing. As I look to my future and the dream of retirement, I want to end up close to my siblings. Truly, Tyler and I have talked about a family compound for years! While we had many times where we tormented each other, the bulk of our upbringing was spent having fun together. When we were little, we would play for hours outside. We would walk through the

Brotherly (and Sisterly) Love

woods and pretend to be frontiersmen like Davy Crockett and Daniel Boone. We would stack pallets together to build our own little home where we would be the Boxcar Children. We would write out menus and play restaurant. We would make up our own rules to board games. We would take our bikes up and down the gravel roads of our neighborhood. We would pile into our little red wagon and race down the hill behind our Grandmama's house. We would write skits and act out plays for our parents. We would sing together. We were never bored. I loved having three other people to have around me all the time.

As we grew older and made friends, we began to do more things separately. As I began dating, I spent more time with my boyfriends. However, every guy I dated knew that there would be many times when my siblings would be going out with us. Not because they had to, but because I really enjoyed being with them. I remember loading them up in my little Subaru and taking them to dollar movies, to the mall for ice cream, or just to drive around while listening to music and slurping milkshakes. When I was finishing high school and looking at college, I chose one that was so close to my parent's house that I could come home every weekend. I even signed up for classes that would allow me to get home on Fridays in time to pick my siblings up from school and would let me have enough time to drive back to school on Monday mornings. I loved (and still love) being a big sister.

As we all became adults and moved on to our own lives, I have never stopped wanting to be the big sister. In my dreamworld, we would all live in walking distance to each other's homes. But that's not the case. Tyler and I live in the same town while Timothy lives in another city, and Andrea lives in another country. Watching them transform into strong, amazing adults who don't necessarily need a big sister around has been sad and rewarding. I am so proud of each of my siblings. I could name attributes and accomplishments aplenty concerning each of them, but what I admire most is their devotion to their faith. They are, without a doubt, huge contributors to my own faith journey. I have learned so much from each of them.

When we were younger, Andrea was always the solid sibling. She never reacted to situations with theatrics. She was always very reasonable. Our family was accident-prone. There was one incident when the four of us were playing outside. My parents were across the road at my Grandmama's house. The layout of our yard was a square with the house creating a border on two sides, one side was open to the driveway, and the fourth side was a steep bank that dropped into a heavily wooded area. Andrea and I were playing together while the boys had taken on a great debate concerning Tarzan … I'm talking about the old-school black-and-white movies where a live-action man was scampering up trees with ease then swinging from limb to limb effortlessly. As the argument became livelier, challenges began to be made. At this time, Tyler was taller than Timothy and was more of a daredevil. Timothy was more of the brains who would think of ideas and figure out how to make one of us test out his theories. If you were to ask Tyler and Timothy what happened, you would get two different accounts, but I think I have enough of the facts to paint an accurate picture. Timothy had taunted Tyler. Tyler reacted by climbing on top of a doghouse to reach the lower

Brotherly (and Sisterly) Love

limb of a tree (probably exactly as Timothy had intended) to show Timothy he could do what Tarzan had done. Name calling and verbal sparring ensued. Timothy, in a hulk-like rage, ran full-force into the doghouse, knocking it down the bank into the woods, with Tyler tumbling over with it. Tyler stands up with blood covering his face because his ear had been severed from his head and was literally dangling by a string of cartilage. Andrea and I watched all of this unfold, and we reacted in two completely different ways. I began screaming at the top of my lungs, and I was certain that Tyler was moments from death. I was yelling at Timothy and trying not to faint. Meanwhile, Andrea calmly walks across the street, gets our parents, and gets the phone to call 9-1-1. This story is one of many where chaos erupts, I panicked, and Andrea was as cool as a cucumber.

In the different seasons of our lives, Andrea has been firm in her faith. When she has had every excuse in the book to say, "why me," she has directed her eyes to Jesus. When trials have faced our family in the most intimate and personal ways, she has always relied on Scripture. Andrea is the person who if she says she will pray for you, she will. She does not waste words. She doesn't put on airs of being hyper-spiritual. She has put in work for years and years to develop her spiritual disciplines. Andrea will tell you that she is not a compassionate or gracious person. She sees herself as someone who reads what the Bible says and does it, and she expects other Christians to do the same. However, I would argue with her. Yes, she may not be an emotional, mushy person, but she prays with sincerity, she shares the perfect words at the perfect time, and she fights for the people she loves. She has challenged me to calm down before I react to a situation. She has pointed me to God's Word more times than I can count. Andrea is a rock. I am so thankful for her faithfulness in my life.

Tyler is probably my most kindred sibling. Of the four of us, I would say he and I are wired the most alike. When we were younger, our parents would pair us up when we would go out and about. The duos were always Tyler and me, then Andrea and Timothy. I have theories as to why our parents sorted us out like this, but to share them here may start a small war within the family. Tyler was my responsibility whenever we would go to the store. He was my seat buddy in the minivan. Even when we had the opportunity to go to Disney World when we were in elementary school, Tyler was my partner. He and I act a lot alike in that we both are talkative, outgoing, and at ease around any person in any amount (I'm losing that part of me the older I get). While Tyler and I share many similarities, he still shines in such a unique way. Tyler has been the person I could always count on to make me smile, no matter the situation. He is honest about his struggles. He is generous beyond measure. Tyler has recently become an elder in our church … one of the youngest ever! I like to call him my younger, elder brother. Tyler has had a life filled with hurt, pain, poor choices, and victories. He is humble about his walk. He is transparent about his struggles. Tyler has challenged me to always show love and grace to everyone, all the time. I can hang on to hurt and shut people out. Tyler fights to let people in. He tries to live his life modeling how Jesus lived his life out in the Gospels. He is so inspiring.

Brotherly (and Sisterly) Love

Timothy and I have had some really special moments together. When he was a junior in high school, he moved in with my husband, toddler, and me several hours from where we grew up. He left behind family and friends to start a new journey to help me and to help him reach some educational goals. During that time, he and I had so much fun together. He was a teenager living with a pregnant sister, toddler niece, and a brother-in-law who was out-to-sea a lot. When I lost one of the babies I was carrying, Timothy sacrificed teenage stuff to sit with me while on bedrest. We would watch movies and television shows. He would drive my little girl and me around in his convertible, blasting 80s rock. He would try to defend me when problems would arise in our little home. He was always standing up for his friends. Even now, so many years later, Timothy remains one of the most determined and strong people I know. When he cares about a person, he gives them all he has. I was so blessed to receive seasons of that attention when I needed it most. As adults, Timothy and I have been able to have many complex discussions about faith. We have argued over sections of Scripture. We have analyzed sermons. Timothy does not allow me to settle or get lazy in my faith. He forces me to stay alert. He pushes me to keep growing.

I know not everyone has grown up with siblings. I know people who have no relationship with their siblings. That's ok. God weaved our family together for a reason, and I believe part of our family's story is in the beauty of the differences in personalities and gifts that work together to strengthen the individual, the family, and then everyone else the family comes in contact with. Being open to learn from the people

Redemptive Grace

God places in our lives is so crucial to personal growth. It would be foolish of me to embrace the mindset that I should be independent. Apparently, God knew I couldn't handle a quiet, isolated life, so He gave me a full house to grow up in. He placed a need in my being to be connected to, surrounded by, and challenged by unique, slightly crazy people. Whether you grew up as an only child, a foster child, an adopted child, in a huge family, or in a completely disconnected family, God wants you to do life with other people. Your family of origin is not the only way to make those connections.

There is an amazing and beautiful thing that happens when a person decides to follow Jesus. When you give your life to Christ, you inherit a huge family. You gain brothers and sisters in the faith all over the world, and all through time! Isn't that mind-bending? To think that your decision to believe that Jesus paid the price for all your wrongdoings connects you to a family network of believers from the Bible to present day to believers who have yet to come to Jesus. I cannot even wrap my little brain around that! So, being a Christian means you have a built-in network of like-minded people facing the battles of life with you. You don't have to be alone. In fact, you are instructed to not take this journey alone. Let's set up camp in the New Testament for a bit.

The beauty of the New Testament is that we can read Jesus' actual words and the instructions written by and for the early church. What amazes me is that everything we read in God's Word is alive and still amazingly applicable centuries after it was written. We'll begin in Matthew 12 where we find Jesus teaching to a crowd and His biological mother and brothers are on the outskirts.

Brotherly (and Sisterly) Love

While Jesus was still talking to the crowd, his mother and brothers stood outside, wanting to speak to Him. Someone told Him, "Your mother and brothers are standing outside wanting to speak to you." He replied to him, "Who is my mother, and who are my brothers?" Pointing to His disciples, He said, "Here are my mother and my brothers. For whoever does the will of my Father in heaven is my brother and sister and mother."

—Matthew 12:46-50

There are many times when I read Jesus' words, and I am taken aback. In our cultural context, we may read these words and think Jesus is being indifferent or dismissive of His actual family. Instead, we need to look deeper and remember that while Jesus was a man, He was still God. He was making a deep point. The notes on these verses from *The Life Application Study Bible* say it best: "… Jesus was pointing out that spiritual relationships are as binding as physical ones, and He was paving the way for a new community of believers (the universal church), our spiritual family" (Zondervan, 2011). Jesus was never focused on the here and now. He was constantly guiding His followers to the future, to eternity. There are many passages of Scripture that speak to caring for one's biological family, but Jesus was trying to convey that the relationships we gain when we gain God as our Father are just as important.

The letter of 1 John was written full of instructions to the early church. One of my most-read passages from 1 John is chapter four. Here, we can read the how and why of being an extended spiritual family. This section has some repetition, but as I say to my children when we read the

Redemptive Grace

Bible, if God has the author use the same word over and over, He is trying to make a point, to get our attention! Stick with it. The first time you read it, do just that. Read it again and underline the repeated words, statements, and ideas. Ready? Here we go!

Dear Friends, let us love one another, for love comes from God. Everyone who loves has been born of God and knows God. Whoever does not love does not know God, because God is love. This is how God showed His love among us: He sent His one and only Son into the world that we might live through Him. This is love: not that we loved God, but that He loved us and sent His Son as an atoning sacrifice for our sins. Dear friends, since God so loved us, we also ought to love one another. No one has ever seen God; but if we love one another, God lives in us, and His love is made complete in us ... We love because He first loved us. Whoever claims to love God yet hates his brother or sister is a liar. For whoever does not love their brother and sister, whom they have seen, cannot love God, whom they have not seen. And He has given us this command: Anyone who loves God must also love their brother and sister."

—1 John 4:7-12,19-21

If you have time, I encourage you to read the verses I omitted from this passage as they are powerful, too; for now, I wanted to focus on the relational components of these specific verses. Use the above passage to answer the following questions. Feel free to use the verses but also write answers in your own words.

Brotherly (and Sisterly) Love

How do we become brothers and sisters in Christ? What joins us together? What is that common bond?

_____

_____

How did God show us His love for us? How do we know He loves us?

_____

_____

Why is it important to love our spiritual brothers and sisters?

_____

_____

What is the command of this passage?

_____

_____

Just like in a biological family, we are going to have highs and lows with our spiritual family. If you have ever been involved with a church family, you have more than likely been in business meetings, heard gossip, been offended by a leader, been disappointed in ministry, etc. The bottom line is that while we are Christ-followers, we are still flawed humans. Newsflash: even the leaders of the church are messed-up, sinful people. They are not perfect. To try and hold them to the same level as Jesus means you absolutely will get disappointed. Fun fact: you and I are not perfect. As conflict arises between brothers and sisters in Christ, we need to keep the command of loving each other at the focus of our hearts and minds. *(There are times when we need to address sin, wrongdoings, etc. with other believers and the Bible tells us how to do that in Matthew 18. There are also times where you may do everything you can to hold on to a church family, but the Holy Spirit leads you elsewhere. That's ok! Just remember to continue to show love to other believers even when you don't agree with them.)* Simply put, we should love them because Christ gave His life for them the same as He did for us. Plus, all the people in our bubbles who don't know Jesus personally are looking to see how we handle conflict within the church! That's a great responsibility!

Take some time to reflect on the relationships you have with your spiritual family. Who are some people who have become "closer than a brother" (Proverbs 18:24)? What is a way you can pour into that relationship this week? I'm a card-writer-sender kind of person; and I love for people to receive happy mail letting them know what they mean to me. Other people are not wordy people. What would make you feel special? Do that for someone else! Write down your who and how here:

Now, here's the hard part. Think about a time (or in my case times) that you may have hurt or been hurt by a spiritual family member. Have you talked with God about it? Have you asked for forgiveness or shown forgiveness? Have you let go of the hurt? Can you find a way to show love again? Now,

Brotherly (and Sisterly) Love

please hear me: there is real pain that can happen in any relationship. People (Christian or not) can cause great hurt. I am asking you to forgive in order for you to heal and for you to be able to progress in your relationship with the Lord. I am not asking you to go back into a situation that causes harm to you. I am a firm believer in love, grace, forgiveness, **and** boundaries. If any of that resonates with you, take this space and this time to give it God and ask for His guidance.

_____

_____

_____

_____

_____

_____

_____

_____

_____

_____

_____

_____

_____

_____

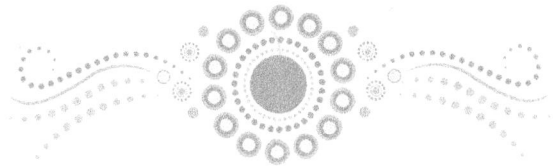

Tainted Love

"Create in me a pure heart…"

—Psalm 51:10

Tackling the subject of marriage is tricky, especially within our culture and even within the church. To write my experience in a transparent light, I feel compelled to address a few things first. Because of the journey I have had, God has given me many opportunities to mentor and counsel women who have been separated or divorced. The Bible has specific verses concerning marriage as well as divorce. While Scripture does say that God hates divorce, He does not hate you. If you are in a relationship that is abusive in any sense of the word, get help, get out. Fighting for a Biblical marriage does not make you a target for abuse or harm. Working on a Christ-centered marriage means both parties are following Jesus, listening to the Holy Spirit, and focusing on God's Word. Someone who is doing these things should not be causing injury to you at the same time. My strongest advice to you if you are in a situation where you feel trapped and in danger is to please be bold and courageous—call a friend, call a church, find local services and hotlines to safely get out of that situation. YOU ARE VALUED! YOU HAVE WORTH! YOU ARE A CHILD OF GOD AND JOINT HEIR OF JESUS! YOU MATTER, so please get out and get help!

Redemptive Grace

Thus far in this book, you have been privy to the vast array of experiences in my life, and you probably have formed a loose timeline. I've mentioned that I married my high school sweetheart when I was nineteen, that he was in the Navy, that we lost two babies, and that we eventually moved back to our hometown. I have shared with you the personal sin struggles of my past, of my need for approval, and of my constant mix-up of living on a works-based faith system. I would like to preface this next section (probably the most personal and vulnerable part of my story) by saying by the grace of God, that even though I am divorced, my ex-husband and I have a good relationship and work together to raise our children. When I share this part of my story, I am not going to give all the details, nor am I going to paint my ex-husband as a villain, because he's not one. I am going to share my struggles, how I contributed to the divorce, and my perspective of having and losing a marriage. Deep breath for me, and here we go. ...

Mark and I met in seventh grade. At that stage in life, I was not really allowed to have a boyfriend, but I did have a lot of friends who were boys. Mark was one of my buddies. In eighth grade, we were in different classes, but when we went on our eighth-grade trip, Mark and I rode go-karts for hours, sat on the bus together and talked, and spent a lot of time laughing and being silly. He asked me to the eighth-grade dance where we had a grown-up dinner, fancy clothes and lots of fun. In high school, Mark and I were in different classes, different extracurriculars and had different friends. It wasn't until eleventh grade that we landed in another class together. He and I were put in a group together

Tainted Love

in our Pre-Calculus class, and from there we renewed our friendship and soon became a couple. Mark came into my life after my confession to my parents, so there were all kind of rules in place to be able to date me including having to attend church with my family. Mark was a good sport. He was the oldest of his siblings, and he understood the responsibility that came with that. For the remainder of our high school years, Mark and I dated, spent time with each other's families, and started planning for a future together. When Mark went to boot camp for the Navy, we broke up because we didn't know what the military life would entail. However, we wrote letters to each other almost every day while he was away. It would take forever to receive letters, and I believed for months that he had forgotten me. When he graduated from boot camp, he invited me to come see the ceremony. I traveled with his family to see him, and there we decided we would do life together.

Through high school and all the medical ordeals I went through, Mark was there for every step. He was always creative, kind, and supportive. One our wedding day, he kept his focus on me. He didn't mind that we had to spend our honeymoon in a hospital. When we moved a thousand miles away from home for him to complete his training, he did his best to provide me with a safe home and fun experiences when he didn't have to work. The Navy moved us a few times, and Mark was great about figuring out ways to have my siblings come and stay with me, especially when he would have to go out on deployment.

Like any union of two people, our marriage had highs and lows. We were able to travel and experience new places.

Redemptive Grace

We both had a heart for taking care of others. Throughout our time in the Navy, we almost always had someone staying in our home. When we would go home to visit, we would want to spend time with our parents, siblings, and grandparents, and we hosted them in our home whenever they were able to come to us. We both enjoyed serving in our church once we stuck with one. We planned events and taught Bible studies together. We had a long history and so many similarities. We also had big lows in our life. Being a military family meant we spent a lot of time apart during the first six years of our marriage. Training, education, overnight watch duties, and deployments were the job. The medical problems I continued to have weighed on our world. The birth of our daughter prematurely and the subsequent health issues and developmental problems she faced was also challenging. Somehow, we managed through those times.

When Mark's time in the Navy was over, he worked for the church we attended. I worked part-time at a school supply store and primarily stayed home with our two little ones. We had lost our son's twin, and that was extremely hard on both of us. During this time, we were still living far away from our hometown. Mark's father had gone through a huge cancer battle. His siblings had started families and moved from home. His parent's marriage was having huge problems. Within the same time span, my parent's marriage was decaying. My siblings were growing up and moving on to university. My Grandmama was battling an aggressive cancer. Our world had gone crazy, and we were hours away from the people we needed and who needed us. We began to talk about moving back home. As those talks were in progress

Tainted Love

and we began looking for jobs and places to live, a hurricane of events took place. My Daddy unexpectedly passed away, Mark's parents and my parents went through divorce, and my Grandmama's health was deteriorating exponentially.

We decided we just had to get home, no matter what. One of our dear friends scouted out homes for us and found us a place to rent in a little town not far from our families. A man we used to go to church with promised Mark a job. It felt like overnight, and we were in a U-Haul driving hours to our new home. Once we arrived, the job Mark had been promised fell through. Both of us were working on our bachelor's degrees (I always say we took the scenic path to an education). I was mainly staying home with our children.

Within a span of around eighteen months, we were bombarded by life. Because Mark was counting on the one job, he had to scramble to find work to provide for us. He took a security guard position that had him working second and third shifts. He was taking classes online to further his education. Our daughter was enrolled in a preschool class where the teacher expressed concerns about her development. After a series of medical and psychological tests, we learned she had a mild form of Cerebral Palsy. I became pregnant again, and we lost that baby. My Grandmama, who was my personal hero, passed away. We weren't actively involved in a church. Our families had so much going on. Mark and I rarely saw each other because of how much he was having to work. Our relationship started to become very quiet. When we did start going to church, we didn't discuss our expectations or comfortability for a new church family. We went where my friend went. The church was different than what we had grown up in and served in, and we had a hard time adjusting, but neither of us talked to each other about it.

Instead of making our marriage a priority, we began to look for ways to improve our personal lives. Mark was able to find another job at a very good company. I started working in a school where our daughter attended and near a preschool for our son. Our lives started to "look" better because our house got bigger, our cars got newer, and we had found a church where we were comfortable and that was so big that we were able to check off our Christian box by just attending. Mark's focus was how to have more, my focus was being a Mama. Neither of us were looking at God's Word, and we definitely weren't taking care of each other. For a couple of years, our marriage took a drastic turn, but we were so honed in on our own stuff, I don't think we realized how deep the damage was.

Each of us brought pain to each other. We never yelled and screamed. Our discussions about anything became less and less. We had friends over every weekend instead of ever taking time out for ourselves or our marriage. We loved hosting people, and in hindsight, I think it was because we had forgotten how to interact with one another, and we were more comfortable together when we had an audience. It was a very quiet marriage. We rarely slept in the same room. We began to do more things independent of one another. I began to have the sins of my past sneak back up into my mind. While working at the school, I had made a dear friend, and I am so thankful for her (we'll get to why)! There was a man who worked at the school, too. Sometimes our lunch breaks would line up with each other. We had a lot in common as far as our professional goals and nerd tendencies would go. The students we cared for often had the same schedule, so our conversations became more frequent. Sin is tricky. In my experience, it's rare that it announces itself in a grand reveal moment. Sin seeps into the brain. It sets up a justification mindset. At home, my husband and I rarely talked to each other, spent most of our time at home separate from each other, and only acted together when we were at church or had friends over. At work, there was someone who told me how smart and pretty and driven I was. We started texting each other. It was ok, because we were both Christians … or, at least that's what I told myself. Our conversations became more personal. Slowly. In my mind, if my husband didn't want me anymore, and someone else did, then it was ok for me to entertain the "grass is greener" thoughts. Thankfully, the amazing friend I mentioned before was a loud voice of reason and truth. She was direct and pointed out what I was toying with. At the same time, Mark was going through his own things, and he had left the kids and me for a few days. For me, this was another greenlight to do what I wanted. But, because of the prayers of my friend, through the unknown prayers of my family members, and because of the Holy Spirit pounding on my heart like a jackhammer, I was able to watch God save me from my sinful self.

I mentioned our daughter's diagnosis and delays. There was a meeting at school with Mark, me, the assistant principal, teachers, and the therapists who worked with our little girl, who was in second grade. During this meeting, we were told she had "plateaued" and wouldn't be able to progress any further. The team wanted to label our daughter "at-risk."

Redemptive Grace

I worked in the "at-risk" classroom, and the children in that class did not have the same issues or needs as our daughter. After talking, Mark and I decided that I would quit my job and homeschool our children. This solved so many issues. This took me out of the workplace where I was being greatly tempted. This allowed me the opportunity to try to get my priorities right as a wife. This gave me the desire of my heart to be home with my babies. I can't speak to all that Mark was processing or doing during this time, and that's not entirely my story to tell anyway. There was a brief honeymoon period where I thought he and I would be ok. We had merged our social media accounts, we were working together to start a business, we were talking about ideas about moving somewhere else to start over. I was in counseling, had joined a women's ministry, and had begun a small job in children's ministry. Mark was working more hours, was working a lot of weekends, and had started taking more frequent business trips. Once again, I shifted my focus on doing what I could do for my kids and me. Mark and I went right back to being roommates, but I had placed every guardrail I could think of around me to keep me from falling back into old thinking.

My sister had moved thousands of miles away and was expecting her first child. Mark, the kids and I packed up to spend time with her and her husband and to hopefully be there when the baby arrived. Our plan was to stay for two weeks. While there, Mark and I looked at jobs in the area, checked out real estate, and talked about moving to be closer to my sister and to start over with each other. After the first week, Mark said he had to go back to work, changed his plane ticket, and left the kids and me with my sister. I was extremely confused, but I was thankful to be near my sister as my nephew was born. The children and I flew back home. I remember getting off the escalator in the airport and Mark standing there looking completely different to me. We drove home. We went back to our routines. One night, after putting the kids to bed, Mark told me he wanted a divorce. I was shocked because I thought things were better because I was doing all the "right" things. I cried. I was sick. I was scared. I was sad.

Over the next few weeks, Mark moved out, and I kicked into hyperdrive in counseling. Mark agreed to come to a few sessions. I would drive to his work and beg him to come home. I confessed to my failures as a wife. I asked him to forgive me. I told him I would do whatever I could to save our family. I kept fighting for our marriage until it became extremely obvious that we would not make it. Over the next year, the separation process, financial struggles and custody battles would take a toll on me. Abandoned. Worthless. Repulsive. Tragic. Unwanted. Fake. These words were my mantra. I poured out my heart to the Lord and asked Him to forgive me. I began to work on my relationship with Jesus. I started being a more consistent spiritual leader to my children. I was alone physically but completely covered by the One who made me.

Now, in our American culture, everything that happened to Mark and me would justify any of our choices. In fact, the state where we live is a "no-fault" state meaning it doesn't matter why a marriage is dissolved, no one is at fault. Our state also does not define marriage as "significant" until it has lasted fifteen years; thirteen doesn't cut it. There were people who didn't know the ins and outs of our marriage, but they

Redemptive Grace

felt they had a right to tell both of us what to do and how to handle the divorce. The biggest regret I have is that initially, I listened to the wrong people and retaliated out of emotions. I remember being in the courtroom after an emotional and brutal attack on me as I fought for custody of my children. I was rarely angry, but I was greatly grieved. In my heart, I felt God tell me to show grace to Mark. Spiritually, he and I were running as fast and hard as we could in completely opposite directions. God reminded me that Mark knew me better than anyone. He knew what I professed to believe. He knew the depths of my sin. He reminded me that I had a choice to be a stumbling block to Mark's faith or to be a source of light pointing Him back to Jesus. That has been the goal of my heart since that moment. Mark and I have been divorced for many years. We are both remarried. We have a custody arrangement that works well for everyone. We can co-parent extremely well. I think that's God's goodness as I try to obey Him. It is still the dream of my heart for Mark to reconnect with Jesus, and I take my role in that extremely seriously. When I adopted the mindset of following God's directive instead of what people thought I should do, I lost several friends. Losing those friends revealed the toxicity I had allowed in my life through people who encouraged justifying my thoughts, who promoted infidelity, and who wanted to see Mark brought to ruin. God reminded me of the true friends and family who were faithful to Him and who became the greatest support system during the bleakest part of my life.

The people who love me best like this chapter least. They say things like, "this makes it sound like you are taking the blame for the divorce. He's the one who wanted the divorce. He's the one that ..." In our case, it took two people for the marriage to fall apart. It was not a quick process. I would absolutely say that the first ten years of our marriage was awesome. I would admit that the road to separation was a slow demise. In the last year, Mark had given up while I was cramming all the "right things" I could in much like a student waiting until the last minute to prepare for a final exam. Yes, I did not want a divorce; however, all I could do and can continue to do is owe my part for the failure of a marriage and give it all back to God whenever the enemy tries to use that phase of my life against me.

This was a loaded portion of my testimony with so many ways to connect to God's Word. Let's start back at the beginning with sin. Each one of us was born with a sin nature. No one had to teach me to mess up. I was already wired that way from day one of my existence. Jesus, God in man, was the only person who was ever without sin. That's just the truth. We have talked about confessing sin, giving our sin to the Lord, asking for forgiveness, and hopefully learning from sin. For me, I absolutely knew the horribleness of what my specific draw to sin was. I had dealt with the consequences earlier in my life. Yet, when my security was in shambles, when my vanity was left wanting, when my femininity was ignored, my brain went right back to my old thoughts. I love to read the letters from Paul in the New Testament. I feel like he just "gets it" ... what it is to be human. Let's go to Romans 7:15-20 and break down this passage together.

Redemptive Grace

"I do not understand what I do. For what I want do I do not do, but what I hate I do. And if I do what I do not want to do, I agree that the law is good. As it is, it is no longer myself who do it, but it is sin living in me. For I know that good itself does not dwell in me, that is, in my sinful nature. For I have the desire to do what is good, but I cannot carry it out. For I do not do the good I want to do, but the evil I do not want to do—this I keep on doing. Now if I do what I do not want to do, it is no longer I who do it, but it is sin living in me that does it."

—Romans 7:15-20

I know this passage has a kind of Dr. Seuss feeling to it, so read it again slowly. How would you summarize these verses? Write them down in your own words here:

_____

_____

_____

My summary would be that I don't know why I sin. I don't understand why I do the things I know I should not do. Because of Jesus in me, I really do want to do what is right and true and holy. Then why do I dance with evil? I do it because I am full of sin, and sin is actively working against me. The enemy is thoroughly pursuing me and wants me to fail.

Well, that's a doomsday thought process, for sure. What can we do? Let's pick up reading in verses 21-25.

"So I find this law at work: Although I want to do good, evil is right there with me. For in my inner being I delight in God's

Tainted Love

law; but I see another law at work in me, waging war against the law of my mind and making me a prisoner of the law of sin at work within me. What a wretched man I am! Who will rescue me from this body that is subject to death? Thanks be to God, who delivers me through Jesus Christ our Lord!"

Oh, my goodness! Who will rescue us? Jesus! Please remember that no matter the sin or brokenness, Jesus is at the ready to hear your confession, to forgive you, and to remind you through His Word of who you are through Him!

A staple in my artillery against sin is this beautiful psalm written by King David after he had committed a series of terrible trespasses. I encourage you to read this as a prayer from your heart to the Lord when you feel your sin nature trying to take over your thoughts and heart. For now, we are just going to look at a few of the verses from this passage. Read them and rewrite them into your own prayer. Let's go to Psalm 51.

Verse 1
"Have mercy on me, O God, according to your unfailing love; according to your great compassion blot out my transgressions."

_____

_____

Verse 2
"Wash away all my iniquity and cleanse me from my sin.

_____

_____

Redemptive Grace

Verse 7

"Cleanse me with hyssop, and I will be clean; wash me, and I will be whiter than snow."

_____

_____

Verse 10

"Create in me a pure heart, O God, and renew a steadfast spirit within me."

_____

_____

Verse 12

"Restore to me the joy of your salvation and grant me a willing spirit, to sustain me."

_____

_____

Oh, my friend, please remember that this is what God wants from you. He wants you to talk with Him, to be honest with Him, to plea with Him. He wants to forgive you and to restore you. He wants to walk with you all day, every day and to help shape you into the amazing person He has designed you to be. Do not let sin be the anchor that weighs you down. Let Jesus clean you up!

This section was extremely transparent for me, and I hope that it spurs you on to reflect on whatever thing you

Tainted Love

are holding onto or battling. I hope you can identify what is the thing that you don't want to do but you keep doing. If nothing comes to mind, I would challenge you to ask God to reveal to you where He sees an opportunity for growth in you. Remember, your issue may not look like mine or anyone else's in your circle. I promise, none of us our perfect or have it figured out. Until we are in heaven with the Creator, we will be battling sin. Please take a few minutes to pour out to God or to beg Him for a revelation in your heart. Write down a prayer to Him to help hold you accountable to yourself!

_____

_____

_____

_____

_____

_____

_____

_____

_____

_____

_____

_____

Redemptive Grace

Because of the heaviness of this chapter, we are going to stop right here. For your homework, I would encourage you to set aside some true quiet time. Go someplace with no distractions. Listen to some praise and worship music. Read Psalm 51. Be quiet. Listen. Be loud. Cry out. Whatever you feel the Holy Spirit is prompting you to do, be intentional about making that time for just the two of you.

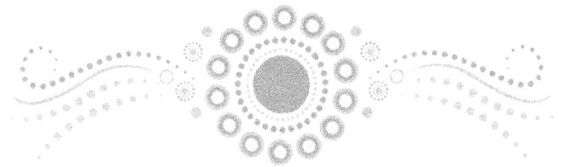

From Wife to Not

"Submit to one another out of reverence for Christ."
—Ephesians 5:21

Recovering from the request for a divorce was an epic battle in my head and heart. As soon as the reality of my husband not coming back was made public, I crumbled. Temptation set its hooks on my mind. I was so sad and extremely lonely. The idea of running away from our hometown was becoming more and more appealing to me. I remember sitting down at the dining room table and pulling up an airline site. I had acquaintances from years gone by who lived far away. I knew that if I went to visit them, I would be blissfully distracted for a week or two. These friends were not believers. They would have been fun to be around, but they would not have stopped me from making decisions that could harm my future. I was so low, that I wasn't thinking past feeling good temporarily. I had my plane ticket in my online cart, had put in my credit card information, had made arrangements with my Mama for my children, and all I had to do was hit the "submit order" button. On the screen, I also had a social media site up as a mindless distraction. In the moment I was about to purchase my ticket and willingly take actions that definitely would have knocked down every guardrail I had put in place in my life, my internet refreshed and there was a new post that I completely believe God had intended for me to see. I'll tell you more about that later, but for now, I will tell you I immediately closed out the airline site and bowed my head and cried. Friends, do not put God in a box. I have read over and over that people wish that God still spoke to us like Moses and the burning bush. I believe He is talking to us all the time. For me, social media was how He got my attention. Slow down in your daily routines and find where He is waiting for you!

I transitioned from being a housewife to a separated woman. I was still primarily a stay-at-home, homeschooling Mom. I was working a few hours a week for our church. I had a new schedule where I had a lot of time alone. At night, after the kids were in bed, I wouldn't know what to do. I love movies, but even I can't stare at a screen indefinitely. I started really reading my Bible more. I started having real conversations with God. I started having honest moments of weeping and pouring out all my pain. God is so good. In those nights when the loneliness felt like an elephant sitting on my shoulders, God would give me gifts. Part of being a Christ-follower means we have access to things like peace that doesn't make sense and joy that continues even when happiness has faded. I hated that time in my life, but I am so grateful for how God shaped me in those late-night sessions.

I have discovered that God is kind. He doesn't guilt-trip. He doesn't overload. He does speak through His Word with compassion and grace. He does protect our hearts and minds. I learned that He reveals things as we can take them in. Initially, my sadness was so strong, that I had a fear that depression followed by suicidal thoughts would overtake me. God knows me. He had me right where He wanted me. I was surrounded by incredible people—an engaged family, a supportive church, amazing friends. He daily reminded me that I was not alone. These like-minded people wrapped me up in their arms and lives. My children and I were greatly cared for. Because of my desire to run into God and not from Him, because I was putting spiritual exercises in place, and because I was doing my best to fight off temptations, I really believe God blessed me with the people who walked through the fire with me.

Even though surrounded by loving people, I still had long hours of solitude. These were the times when I could clearly hear God speak to me. This is when He would reveal to me the areas where I needed to work, grow, and change. This is when He would show me where I had failed as a wife. Oh, how my thoughts changed. I was ready to learn. I wanted to be shaped into something new, something better. I wanted God to use me. The initial lessons during these quiet times directly spoke of marriage. Since I had been a key player in tearing one down, I wanted to grow to be someone who advocated for Biblical marriage. I knew this was the time for my testimony to take a new turn. This is when I felt the call on my life to be transparent.

Maybe you've been married for a lifetime. Maybe you're newly married. Maybe you're single. Maybe you're separated or divorced. Maybe you're on your next marriage. Maybe marriage isn't on your radar at the present. Maybe marriage isn't a desire of your heart. All of those are acceptable places to be! Regardless of where you are on the scale, it is important to understand what the Bible says about marriage because you will more than likely be dealing with married people;

more importantly, knowing what marriage should represent to all believers is a beautiful thing! What is Biblical marriage? Let's get into the Word!

"Then the Lord God formed man from the dust of the ground and breathed into his nostrils the breath of life, and the man became a living being."

—Genesis 2:7

"The Lord God said, 'It is not good for the man to be alone. I will make a helper suitable for him.'"

—Genesis 2:18

"But for Adam no suitable helper was found. So the Lord God caused the man to fall into a deep sleep; and while he was sleeping, he took one of the man's ribs and then closed up the place with flesh. Then the Lord God made a woman from the rib he had taken out of the mand, and he brought her to the man. The man said, 'This now bone of my bones and flesh of my flesh; she shall be called woman, for she was taken out of a man.' This is why a man leaves his father and mother and is united to his wife, and they become one flesh."

—Genesis 2:20b-24

In the very beginning of everything, God used His amazing creativity to bring man to life and to bring man and woman together. Reading this passage promotes such incredible imagery. I imagine that Adam was probably not bored with all the tasks God had given him. I like to think he enjoyed naming the animals and spending time with the

From Wife to Not

Creator. Since this is before sin has entered the world, we can assume Adam wasn't sad or lonely, but I do imagine that there was a thrill that ran through him when he saw Eve for the first time. Here was someone designed just for him, to compliment him, to help him, to do life with him. What joy must have been present in the garden when God revealed His creation of woman to His creation of man! So, here, at the start of all things, God establishes a beautiful bond between two people. He also establishes some expectations. We read further in Genesis 2 that God had given Adam a hefty chore list of caring for the garden and its inhabitants. He also gave Adam a paradise to explore and enjoy. Adam has a lot of responsibility. Enter Eve. God brought her to the picture to be on Adam's team, to support him, and to help him.

What is your understanding of Biblical marriage? How have the churches, Bible studies, small groups, etc. influenced your view of marriage?

_____

_____

What is your family history of marriage? Are there members of your family who have been together a hundred years? Are there many divorces in your family? How has your family's treatment of marriage affected your thoughts on marriage?

_____

_____

Redemptive Grace

Have you had Biblical marriage modeled for you? If so, by whom?

_____

_____

Matthew Henry stated it best in his commentary of Genesis: *"Women were created from the rib of man to be beside him, not from his head to top him, nor from his feet to be trampled by him, but from under his arm to be protected by him, near to his heart to be loved by him" (Henry, 1706)*. What does this quote make you feel and think about marriage? Rewrite his words as your own.

_____

_____

_____

_____

When you read the word "submission," what comes to mind? What does submission mean to you? Who should you submit to?

_____

_____

Through my journey in life, through the various churches I attended and Bible studies I participated in, I had never fully understood Biblical submission until I went

From Wife to Not

through my divorce. When I was growing up in the Southern Baptist church, divorce was not talked about. If someone in the congregation was divorced, they were often the topic of gossip or unkind treatment. Shame on us, church. As my family moved around and were involved in different churches, I found the same thing to be true. Divorce was taboo. And what the young women were being taught about submission was not entirely accurate, although I am sure it was well-intended. What we're going to do next is read several passages of Scripture and reflect on what the Bible says about marriage and submission.

Married Couples—(Disclaimer, the following apply to married couples. If you are single, dating, or engaged, your job is to keep the focus on your relationship with Jesus. If you choose to get married, please find a Christian premarital counselor who will guide you into the transition of going from single to engaged to married.)

To help me better grasp heavy topics in Scripture, I use the *Life Application Study Bible*. The breakdown of each verse is extremely helpful, and there are topical notes as well. Here is what the LASB says about submission: *"Submission is functional (a distinguishing of our roles and the work we are called to do); relational (a loving acknowledgement of another's value as a person); reciprocal (a mutual, humble cooperation with one another); universal (an acknowledgement by the church of the all-encompassing lordship of Jesus Christ)"* (Zondervan, 2011). With those keys in mind, let's go to the New Testament.

"Submit to one another out of reverence for Christ."
—Ephesians 5:21

Redemptive Grace

This verse is very clear, yet the modern church seems to get it confused. We are not to submit to our husband or wife for any reason other than honoring Christ. That's it. Because of the church's history and the scandalous examples that take up headlines when addressing Christianity and submission, the heart of this union has become perverse. We should submit to our spouse because of Jesus. Jesus submitted to God. He willingly gave us His life because God asked it of Him. It's not about who is in control, it is about trying to be more like Jesus.

Wives

"Wives, submit yourselves to your own husbands as you do to the Lord. For the husband is the head of the wife as Christ is the head of the church, His body, of which He is the Savior. Now as the church submits to Christ, so also wives should submit to their husbands in everything."

—Ephesians 5:22-24

In my church experience, I was taught to be submissive to my husband, and that was it. There was no reading the rest of the verse. Submission was projected as blind obedience. No matter what my husband did or said, it was the right thing, and my job was to respect him and support him. When we take the time to read all the verses, proverbial light bulbs should be illuminating over our heads! Wives should submit as they submit to the Lord. Translation, am I doing for my husband what I do for Jesus? There was a season of my life where I was praying, reading the Bible, teaching my children, but I was doing nothing for my husband. Whoa. Essentially, we were two people with our own sets of responsibilities, our own calendars, our own alone time, and none of it was filtered through Jesus. We were both in self-preservation mode.

"Wives, in the same way submit yourselves to your own husbands so that, if any of them do not believe the word, they may be won over without words by the behavior of their wives, when they see the purity and reverence of your lives. [Your beauty] should be that of your inner self, the unfading beauty of a gentle and quiet spirit, which is of great worth in God's sight."
—I Peter 3:1-2,4

There are other passages in the Bible that tell Christ-followers to not be 'unequally yoked' or married to someone who does not believe. However, there are those who may have committed to marriage before committing to Jesus, there are those who may have spouses who have fallen away from the faith, and there are countless relational issues that would merit application of these verses. Regardless of where a husband's spiritual walk is, wives are told here to use actions to showcase Jesus to their husbands. We've all heard "actions speak louder than words." The LASB states this clearly: *"Submission is voluntarily cooperating with someone, first out of love and respect for God and then out of love and respect for that person. Submitting to unbelievers is difficult, but it is a vital part of leading them to Jesus Christ. We are not called to submit to nonbelievers to the point we compromise our relationship with God, but we must look for every opportunity to humbly serve in the power of God's Spirit"* (Zondervan, 2011).

Redemptive Grace

We need to have our priorities in place. First, we submit to God, then to our spouse.

How do your actions measure up to this passage? Are you showing your husband Jesus' love? If so, that means you are sharing grace, forgiveness, patience, gratitude, and all those wonderful gifts that Christ gives us. How's your attitude? Is it pure, gentle, and quiet? If you aren't married right now, you can still answer. What is your attitude in dealing with others? Do you have a quiet spirit, pure thoughts, a gentle demeanor? Now, this is not saying that once we are married, we morph into Christian-Stepford Wives. God made each of us uniquely and purposefully. We can still be who we were created to be, but our attitude should reflect Jesus no matter how we are wired. When the tone of our heart is right, we are beautiful! Use the space below to reflect on the following questions: What kind of wife am I? What kind of wife do I want to be? How can I incorporate Jesus' love in my attitude? Write down 3-5 steps you can take to develop or improve your attitude!

1. _____

_____

2. _____

_____

3. _____

_____

From Wife to Not

4. _____

_____

5. _____

_____

Husbands

"Husbands, love your wives, just as Christ loved the church and gave Himself up for her to make her holy, cleansing her by the washing with water through the word, and to present her to Himself as a radiant church, without stain or wrinkle or any blemish, but holy and blameless. In this same way, husbands ought to love their wives as their own bodies. He who loves his wife loves himself. After all, no one ever hated their own body, but they feed it and care for their body, just as Christ does the church—for we are members of His body."

—Ephesians 5:25-30

Paul spends a lot of time here talking about Christ's relationship to the church. He uses this to show husbands how they should treat their wives. As we read these verses, we should think back to what Jesus did for each of us. He gave up Heaven. He was born into poverty. He grew up as each of us did. He walked this earth and was tempted as we are. He knew the only way for people to be reconciled and given the opportunity of eternal life with God was to willingly give up His own life. He was perfection sacrificed for selfish, sin-filled people. Even so, He loved us. When I look back over my story and the contents of my heart, I am disgusted with myself. Jesus knows all about me, and He still gave everything up for me. I do not get it … no matter how much I read and pray, I don't understand. All I can do is accept the gift of His saving grace. Husbands are told to be of that same mind. A husband is called to love and care for his bride the way Jesus loves His people.

"Husbands, in the same way be considerate as you live with your wives, and treat them with respect as the weaker partner and as heirs with you of the gracious gift of life, so that nothing will hinder your prayers."

—I Peter 3:7

Wow! For such a short verse, this is packed with significance. The phrase "weaker partner" or "weaker vessel" in other interpretations, often causes women to shut down and gloss over this passage. *"Peter's mention of the wife as the "weaker" partner is not an insult toward women or a statement of moral or spiritual superiority of men (as some throughout church history have claimed). "Weaker" refers instead to the fact that women are generally physically weaker than men, and so a husband's role is to ensure that his wife is protected, cared for, and treated with dignity and honor" (Strauss, 2016).* If you grew up under the teaching I did, you may have the misconception that somehow women were "less than" in a marriage relationship and that men were in power. What Peter is showing us is the men and women are both receivers of "the gift of life" through Jesus. He is also revealing that prayers can be hindered if the husband is not following God's directions for leadership. This should translate into a team mentality in a marriage. The husband and wife should be rooting for each other. The husband has the responsibility and the call to lead the wife. The wife should be doing everything in her power to cheer on and promote the husband. They both should be honoring Christ first and each other second. When the line-up is right, even the most difficult decisions can be made together bringing glory to God and strengthening the marriage relationship!

The Western view of marriage is so skewed, and our culture places little value on the sanctity of marriage. If you "fall out of love," if you don't want to be married anymore, if you've grown apart, or if you've found love with someone else, then ending your marriage is perfectly acceptable to mainstream America. This is heartbreaking! If you and your spouse are working on having a Biblical marriage, this will not make sense to the secular world. A Biblical marriage rooted in mutual submission and respect that does not give up or give in easily goes against everything in our society. Marriage is so important because it shows a broken world what Jesus did for humanity! Let's look back at Ephesians:

"For this reason a man will leave his father and mother and be united to his wife, and the two will become one flesh. This is a profound mystery—but I am talking about Christ and the church."
— Ephesians 5:31-32

Can you see the correlation between the marriage relationship between husband and wife with the relationship between Christ and the church? It's a mystery. It doesn't make sense. Especially to those who do not follow Jesus. When we accept Christ as our Savior, we are giving up ourselves. When we attempt to live holy lives, we are giving up our selfish ways. When we work toward daily submitting to God's will, we are saying no to our own desires. In the same way, a marriage relationship should model this concept to the world. When a husband puts the needs of his wife ahead of his own, when a wife lavishes her husband with respect, when the two work together to solve the issues of life, they are following God's plan and showing everyone else a love and lifestyle that is not easy and does not make sense! Pastor Chris Dillon summarized this topic best: *"Submission is a weapon for good in God's Kingdom. Apart from the Gospel, submission does not make sense ... it is counter-cultural but critical"* (Dillon, 2020). When we choose to follow Christ, our decisions will be confusing to others, but taking on that lifestyle is our greatest tool in showing Jesus to a world who desperately needs Him. The marriage relationship is essential in making that connection in the minds of lost family and friends.

After reading these passages, what are your thoughts on Biblical submission? Write out your own definition below:

_____

_____

_____

What is a way you can submit to Jesus? What are some things you can do to submit to your spouse (whether married or as you think ahead)?

From Wife to Not

_____

_____

_____

_____

What is the purpose of Biblical submission? How can a Biblical marriage relationship show others the message of the Gospel?

_____

_____

If you are married, how would you rate your marriage as one based on Christ's example? What can you do to improve your score? Don't be discouraged. Instead, be encouraged that God wants to use you and your spouse to help Him showcase His love for the world!

_____

_____

If you are not married, what are some fears you have about Biblical submission and marriage? How can you combat those fears?

_____

_____

_____

Redemptive Grace

I'd like to end this section with some reminders of what submission is not, courtesy of Pastor Chris Dillon. **Biblical submission is not:**

- teaching that all women are to submit to all men. Men and women are of equal value and worth. Wives are to submit to Christ first!
- teaching that women are inferior to men. Christian men are commanded to love, serve, and give up their lives for their wife. Christian men are to lead spiritually.
- about superiority.
- teaching that women are doormats.
- passive, not timid.
- teaching that women are spiritually weak or less intelligent.
- teaching that men should use physical strength to hurt, dominate, intimidate, or abuse. A man's strength should be used to honor, protect, and shield his wife. (Dillon, 2020).

Again, if you are in danger, suffering from abuse of any kind, are scared, etc. PLEASE know that you are LOVED, CHOSEN, and VALUED by God. You are His daughter. He is not a God of fear. He does not want you to live a life of "less than." Please reach out to your local authorities if you are in danger. Reach out to a local Christ-following, Gospel-centered church. Get out!!!

Redemptive Grace

"Let the redeemed of the Lord tell their story ... and tell of His works with songs of joy ..."
—Psalm 107:2

At the beginning of the last chapter, I mentioned a social media post that redirected my thoughts, and that I fully believe was God-ordained. When I was planning to run away from my hurt and pain, God got my attention through another believer. My husband and I had a shared social media account before he left. We had a friends list made up from people he and I both knew, most of which were from our high school days and from the church we attended. What I knew of the author of the post that changed my life was that he loved God, loved Notre Dame, was super-involved in the church, was in a men's group with Mark, was divorced and had two daughters. He would often post funny things or about missing his girls when they were with their mom. That was the extent of my knowledge of this guy. What I didn't know is that his youngest daughter and my daughter had become friends at church! This is very important later on.

The post-writer's name was Brian, and this is what he had written, "Drove around a lot last night thinking about everything leading up to now in my life—some things have been great, some things have been horrible. But at the end of the day, all I can focus on is how many great things that God has blessed me with, and the things that were bad, are in my past for a reason, so I think I'll just leave them there—where they belong." I knew Brian had been married and that he was a dad. In the center of my hurt, I did not understand how someone could have such an optimistic, God-focused outlook. All I knew was I felt abandoned, worthless, and isolated. It made no sense to me how this guy, who had been where I was, was talking about leaving his past behind him and trusting God with his future. How could he still trust a God who had let his marriage fall apart? How could he trust a God who allowed him to be separated from his children on a weekly basis? This was a complete mystery to me. My brain was shifting to believing God really didn't care about my world at all. I had to get answers.

Now, I am a friendly person. In my younger days, I was outgoing and extroverted. Through my separation, I found myself becoming more reserved and introspective, but still friendly. And, as we have learned, I have a tendency to fall into works-based salvation, which draws me to following all the right social rules, especially in a church setting. However, I was desperate to know how this man who had walked where I had was not angry and bitter. I needed to understand how his faith had not been shattered. I jumped out of my comfort zone and messaged Brian on social media. Let me be very clear—I did not message him out of loneliness, looking for companionship, or anything relationship-minded. I messaged him to ask if he could please tell me how he survived what I was struggling to process. While we attended the same church, our Sunday mornings were spent on different cam-

Redemptive Grace

puses. Because of my friend and pastor, my role working for the church was growing, and I was spending Sundays at the main campus learning the ropes of ministry. Brian suggested meeting at the coffee counter … very public, very busy and very appropriate. At this point, he had no idea who I was other than someone who attended the same church. To his knowledge, I was happily married. (Isn't it interesting the personas we present in the social media world. This is why it is so important for each of us to remember that we have no idea what goes on in homes offline!)

When I introduced myself to Brian at the coffee counter, I asked, "how do you do it? How are you not angry and bitter and ready to explode?." I told him what had happened, and he was "floored." He told me that what had gotten him through was realizing that God was bigger than his problems. Consequently, he sent me a link to his video interview where he had shared a portion of his story for a sermon series. As he spoke in that interview, I felt such relief. Brian had been exactly where I was standing, and he had made it! I told Brian I used to listen to his interview every night when I was trying to go to sleep. I would repeat the last words he spoke over and over in my mind and heart: "God never fails. He never gives up on you. God fights for you." The truth of who God is and that He absolutely cares for His children was what I needed to focus on. This is what led me to start reading through the Psalms and crying out to God during my lonely nights.

So many changes hit my world during this time. I went from being a stay-at-home Mom, homeschooling my two children to working full-time for our church, which was a complete blessing financially for me. This was the first job I had ever had that allowed me to take care of myself and my children. I had benefits. I had friends and support. I had great coworkers. God provided for me and my children in such an amazing way! The tradeoff for working full-time was that my children would have to go to public school. This was not the plan when I became a mom, but we had to adapt because I had to have an income. I had no credit because everything had been under my first husband's name, so finding a new home was challenging. Again, I had no choice. When the bank sends the big man to your house to tell you to get out or he'll drag you out, you figure out what to do. I spent two days driving all over our town looking for a place to live. God provided us with an apartment I could afford. The lady in the office was a fellow believer, and she worked with me to complete the paperwork to make it possible to rent my own place for my children and me. My children and I went through our big house and figured out what would fit in our little apartment. Looking back, the time in the apartment was precious. The three of us took on the transitions in our lives with a lot of pain and uncertainty, but we had one another, and we were serving a big God who kept reminding us of how much He loved us.

Remember how I told you my daughter and Brian's daughter (Hannah) had been friends at church? Unbeknownst to me, Brian and Hannah had been involved in setting up the smaller church campus where I would ultimately work. Hannah and Cecely (my daughter) had met in children's ministry and had become fast friends. After the new campus was ready to operate, Brian and Hannah went back to the main campus. When summer rolled around and it was time for

Redemptive Grace

Vacation Bible School, one of my responsibilities was getting the children from the secondary campus to the main campus. One morning while checking in all the children in the big lobby, I heard Cecely squeal and see her rush off across the room. She and Hannah were running to each other like long lost friends! It was a sweet sight to behold, but I had no idea the two of them knew each other, and I had only ever seen Hannah on social media posts with her Dad. Over the course of the week, the two of them reconnected, and the next thing I knew was Cecely was asking for Hannah to come spend the night. Living in the apartment complex had its perks. We had access to an incredible swimming pool and super cool movie room. The three of us used the amenities all the time, and we often had extra kiddos with us!

During this season of my life, I was completely content with my life being my children and me. I had no desire for romance. I definitely had no goal or dream of being a wife again. I had nothing in me wanting to even think about trust or intimacy or love or any of it. I was content working and being with my babies. When they would visit their dad, I would busy myself with Bible studies or spend time at my friends' homes. The thought of letting another man in my life was not even on the radar.

As the summer progressed, Hannah was spending most of her weekends at the pool with my kiddos. This would often lead to sleepovers. If you recall from the beginning of this book, I love a full, noisy home. I would have 1-4 extra kiddos in my home most weekends, and I absolutely loved it! One day as we were planning another pool and movie night, Hannah asked if her Dad could come over to swim and watch

Redemptive Grace

a movie with us. Now, Brian and I were in contact, but it was random, platonic, and usually messages or posts in social media concerning funny video clips, inspirational songs, or a Bible verse. I honestly believed that I would be single forever and that I was too damaged to be redeemed. Brian had sworn off dating completely. He had told God, "I'm done ... if you have someone for me, you'll have to bring them to me."

Brian and I ended up in a couple of small groups together, and through those encounters, we learned a lot about each other. This opened us up for conversations on deeper levels about our pasts, our spirituality, our beliefs, our goals, and our dreams. We talked a lot, we laughed nonstop. We spent time with each other when our kids were hanging out, at church functions, or in small groups. After a significant amount of time passed, Brian and I began to date. We both felt we were too old for a casual relationship, but we didn't want to end up hurt or alone again. We decided to take on counseling, and what a gift that was. Our counselor was the most patient, wise, caring, and thoughtful person. Those sessions were extremely intense and difficult, and there were many days when I wanted to walk out and slam the door. Counseling made me feel exposed and vulnerable, which were the last things I wanted to experience again. Our counselor guided us through God's Word and prayer and helped us understand and process what we were taking on in joining our broken lives together. Brian and I had very similar divorce stories. While that made us empathetic towards each other, it also meant that we had the same baggage and insecurities.

We've been married for several years now, and I have a billion stories I could share about the ups and downs of

Redemptive Grace

blending a family and being a second wife. (Maybe that's another book!) The purpose of this part of my story is to remind each of us how God is a God who reconciles, restores, and redeems. He is a good God who is in all the details of our lives. He is the Creator who designed each person with a purpose and for a purpose. He is a God who wants to hear from us and who wants to speak to us. He loves us so very much. He loves you! In the pain of life, we can often forget the truths about the One who made us. We can feel heavy with doubt, numb with indifference, stalled out in the unknown, stopped by fear, trapped by worry. … Remember who the enemy is. Satan wants you to revel in those lies. He wants you to give up. I'm here to challenge you to fight the enemy for your heart and mind! Reconnect with the One who loved and loves you on the deepest most intimate levels! You can be reconciled! You can be restored! You can be redeemed!

In my darkest days and nights, I would rely on the words of psalmists. There were times when I could not form sentences, or I would be so grief-stricken that I could not even speak. I would weep and moan. I would refer to the Psalms and pour out the words that had already been written in an attempt to feel something or hear something from God. When I cried out, He met me where I was. I could hear Him through Scripture. I could feel Him in the peace, joy, and strength in my soul. Let's look to the Bible to make a plan to climb out of the pit the next time we are knocked down in life.

Psalm 71
n you, Lord, I have taken refuge, let me never be put to shame. In your righteousness, rescue me and deliver me; turn your

Redemptive Grace

ear to me and save me. Be my rock of refuge, to which I can always go; give the command to save me, for you are my rock and fortress. Deliver me, my God from the hand of the wicked, for the grasp of those who are evil and cruel.

For you have been my hope, Sovereign Lord, my confidence since my youth. From birth, I have relied on you; you brought me forth from my mother's womb. I will ever praise you. I have become a sign to many; you are my strong refuge. My mouth is filled with your praise, declaring your splendor all day long.

Do not cast me away when I am old; do not forsake me when my strength is gone. For my enemies speak against me; those who wait to kill me conspire together. They say, "God has forsaken him; pursue him and seize him, for no one will rescue him." Do not be far from me, my God; come quickly, God, to help me. May my accusers perish in shame; may those who want to harm me be covered with scorn and disgrace.

As for me, I will always have hope; I will praise you more and more. My mouth will tell of your righteous deeds, of your saving acts all day long—though I know not how to relate them all. I will come and proclaim your mighty acts, Sovereign Lord; I will proclaim your righteous deeds, yours alone. Since my youth, God, you have taught me, and to this day I declare your marvelous deeds. Even when I am old and gray, do not forsake me, my God, till I declare your power to the next generation, your mighty acts to all who are to come.

Your righteousness, God, reaches to the heavens, you who have done great things. Who is like you God? Though you have made me see troubles, many and bitter, you will restore my life again;

Redemptive Grace

from the depths of the earth, you will again bring me up. You will increase my honor and comfort me once more.

I will praise you with the harp for your faithfulness, my God; I will sing praise to you with the lyre, Holy One of Israel. My lips will shout for joy when I sing praise to you—I whom you have delivered. My tongue will tell of your righteous acts all day long, for those who wanted to harm me have been put to shame and confusion.

I love this Psalm because it seems to cover everything. Real pain can be heard in the author's words. He is desperate and broken, but he is also honest and transparent. Over the course of this song, the author cries out to God and showcases the reasons for his pain; yet he also acknowledges the constant faithfulness of God. In the trial, he is still praising God. We don't have to pray single prayers addressing one thing at a time. Prayer is a conversation with the Lord. I always say He knows what I'm thinking, so I might as well put it all out there! This prayer is all over the emotional map, and that is ok! There is not a formula to communicate with God. Just be open and honest. He will meet you where you are. Read Psalm 71 again and underline the words that relate to you where you are right now. Pray this prayer out loud. Be bold! Be honest!

Isaiah 4:3-4, 9-10
"Listen to me, you descendants of Jacob, all the remnant of the people of Israel, you whom I have upheld since your birth, and have carried since you were born. Even to your old age

Redemptive Grace

and gray hairs I am he, I am he who will sustain you. I have made you and I will carry you; I will sustain you and I will rescue you ...

Remember the former things of long ago; I am God, and there is no other; I am God, and there is none like me. I make known the end from the beginning, from ancient times, what is still to come. I say 'My purpose will stand, and I will do all that I please.' ...

This passage was another one that I clung to. God is speaking to His chosen people. He is reminding them of who He is and of His strength, power, and intentionality. The strong language of these verses helps me to remember that God is for me and that there is nothing He cannot do! He wants each of us to live our lives in His power and for His purpose.

Are there other Scripture passages or songs that you hold on to? If so, write them here. Use this book as a tool to help you remember from whence you have come and to help you fight the good fight, run the race, and remember that God is with you and for you!

In closing, friends, I hope you have been encouraged and inspired. I hope you have been reminded that you are greatly love. I hope you have found the strength and vulnerability to find your own story of redemptive grace!

References

Child Evangelism Fellowship. www.cefonline.com

Dillon, Chris. "Hope in Exile." June 28, July 5, 2020. New Life Community Church, Asheville, NC. Sermon.

Genesis 2 Commentary—Matthew Henry Commentary on the Whole Bible (Complete). (n.d.). Retrieved February 02, 2021, from https://www.biblestudytools.com/commentaries/matthew-henry-complete/genesis/2.html

Getty, K. & Townend, S. (2002). *In Christ Alone.* Thank You Music, LTD. Capitol Christian Music Group Publishing.

Life application study Bible: New International Version. (2011). Grand Rapids, MI: Zondervan Pub. House.

Longman, T. (2015). *Layman's Old Testament Bible commentary: Easy-to-understand insights into Genesis through Malachi.* Uhrichsville, OH: Barbour Books.

Strauss, M. (2016). *Layman's New Testament Bible commentary: Easy-to-understand Insights into Matthew through Revelation / consulting editor Dr. Mark Strauss.* Uhrichville, OH: Barbour Books.

www.ingramcontent.com/pod-product-compliance
Lightning Source LLC
Chambersburg PA
CBHW070155100426
42743CB00013B/2917